THE ART
of
PRACTISING
THE
VIOLIN

THE ART
OF
PRACTISING THE VIOLIN

With Useful Hints for All String Players

by

ROBERT GERLE

Stainer & Bell, London

First published in Great Britain by
Stainer & Bell Ltd, 23 Gruneisen Road, London N3 1DZ
Second Edition 1985
Reprinted 1990, 1995, 2000, 2003

Gerle, Robert
    The art of practising the violin.
    1. Violin
    I. title
    787.1′07′14   MT262

    ISBN 0-85249-506-4

Printed in Great Britain by Caligraving Ltd, Thetford, Norfolk

Photograph by Christian Steiner. Used with permission.

Robert Gerle

Robert Gerle began to study in the Liszt Academy in Budapest at an early age in the class of Geza de Kresz, who was himself a pupil of Hubay, Sevcik and Ysaÿe and a close friend of Flesch, Thibaud and Enesco. He has therefore a thoroughbred technical 'pedigree'.

As a performer, he first won international recognition as a prizewinner in the Thibaud and Geneva Competitions immediately after the Second World War and began the first of many major concert tours in Europe, including solo appearances with the Berlin Philharmonic and the London Royal Philharmonic.

In the 1950s, Robert Gerle was invited by Paul Rolland to the University of Illinois, where he worked with Georges Enesco. He remained closely associated with Rolland, playing for part of the latter's famous film series on violin technique now widely used both in America and England.

This book comes from long experience as a teacher in many notable American conservatoires (including Manhattan, Peabody and Mannes) and universities such as Southern California, Oklahoma and Ohio. He is now Professor of Music and Head of the Instrumental Program in the University of Maryland, at Baltimore (UMBC).

Combining his teaching with playing and conducting, Robert Gerle includes in his recorded repertoire concertos by Barber, Berg, Delius, Hindemith and Kurt Weill as well as classics such as the Beethoven sonatas (with his wife, Marilyn Neeley) and Vieuxtemps concerto. His conducting engagements regularly take him to Canada and South America as well as guest dates in the United States. The convictions expressed in this book show him to be truly one of America's outstanding string teachers.

CONTENTS

To Marilyn
the inspiring example and proof
that
good practice does make perfect

FOREWORD

Go on; don't only practise your art, but force your
way into its secrets; art deserves that, for it and
knowledge can raise man to the Divine.

BEETHOVEN
Letter to a young friend, quoted in
Grove, *Beethoven and his Nine Symphonies*
(Novello, London, 1898)

One of the most important things an aspiring performer can learn during his
formative years is how to use his practice time productively.

Practice is teaching yourself to be student and teacher at the same time; and
success depends to a great extent on how well you teach yourself. Someone else
can tell you and show you how to play the instrument, or inspire you by a
beautiful interpretation. Indeed, an able teacher is indispensable to serve as a
guide and adviser in our progress. But even then, as performers, we still have to
do our own practising ourselves, most of the time alone and without help:
ultimately only the player can 'teach' himself the actual means of playing and
performing.

It is of course essential to learn the fundamentals of basic violin technique,
and to learn them correctly. But it is equally important to know what to do with
this skill, how to maintain it, develop it, and how to apply it in the service of
musical performance and interpretation. It takes a thoughtful and carefully
organized practice method to do this successfully: to make productive use of
valuable practice time; to maintain technical proficiency on a consistently high
level; to keep in hand, and to enlarge, your share of the constantly growing
repertoire; and to keep alive that enthusiasm and inspiration without which
any performance is a mere recitation of notes.

A great many books have already been written on how to play the violin
according to the particular principles of the various schools of violin playing.
In contrast, the art of practising—an art which is equally valid for all schools of
playing—has been given very little attention as a subject in itself. And yet, all
too often what passes for practising is nothing more than the endless and
mindless repetition of the same passage, usually with the same mistakes. This is
a waste of time which does not lead to improvement, only frustration: you
merely learn your mistakes better.

The purpose of this book is to show the way toward better practice habits, to
serve as a guide in the better use of time alone with the instrument, to help

learning more thoroughly, and to retain more lastingly. It stimulates thinking during practice so that you need not worry during the performance; with intelligent practice, the performance can become all the more spontaneous.

Although the examples are all given for violin, almost all the advice in the book applies equally to the viola; and cello and bass students will find a great many of the general hints useful. To some readers, some of the principles formulated in this book may sound familiar; to all, however, even one or two new and helpful ideas may lead to a significant improvement in practice technique...and so raise your performance, if not to the divine level that Beethoven would wish, at least beyond its present limits.

ACKNOWLEDGMENTS

I would like to pay tribute to the memory of the great musicians with whom I had the privilege of studying over the years and whose influence and inspiration is, I hope, reflected in this book: to my professors at the Franz Liszt Academy of Music in Budapest, Géza de Kresz, Imre Waldbauer, Leo Weiner and Zoltán Kodály; and to my mentors later in the United States, Paul Rolland, Georges Enesco, Gregor Piatigorsky and Serge Koussevitzky.

I would also like to express my special appreciation to Dr. Allen Percival, CBE, for his invaluable advice and contributions to the editing of this book, and my sincere thanks to Mr. Donald Waxman of New York City for his initial encouragement and assistance.

I am grateful to the following for permission to quote from copyright material:

Oxford University Press:
I. M. Yampolsky, *The Principles of Violin Fingering*, translated by Alan Lumsden (London, 1967)

Simon and Schuster:
Eduard Hanslick, *Vienna's Golden Years of Music, 1850–1900*, translated and edited by Henry Pleasants III (New York, 1950)

Baltimore, 1982   Robert Gerle

INTRODUCTION

All instrumentalists, amateur or professional, have in common these days the steadily diminishing amount of time they can spend practising, and the need to make the best use of it.

This lack of practice time is due to a number of gradual, but relentless changes in the sociological climate of our time. The relatively short period since the end of World War II in 1945 has seen a dramatic expansion of the mass media and telecommunications: television, telephone, radio and movies, newspapers by computers and broadcasts by satellites. This progress has made every kind of entertainment all too readily available for a large number of people and its easy appeal is making much greater inroads on everybody's time than was the case only a few years ago.

The ever greater and faster travel facilities have enlarged everyone's range of activities, extended circles of acquaintances and made previously unheard-of concert schedules possible. Today, with all these outside pressures, it is more and more difficult for even the most dedicated and single minded musician to find two or three hours' worth of undisturbed and uninterrupted practice time.

Other sociological changes have also contributed to this state of affairs, especially for the younger generation. At an early age, when the commitment for a musical career needs to be made, the parents' influence and guidance is strong and decisive. Their tendency is to urge even the most talented youngster to pursue a full-time degree course of academic studies (with all the classwork it entails) along with their musical studies: a college degree is felt to provide some measure of security which the unpredictability of the musical profession may not always do. In the absence of a systematic and nationwide talent-search, too many talented youngsters start serious music studies too late—particularly string players. Then, rising tuition costs and disappearing scholarship funds are also forcing more and more college students all over the world to work at least part-time in order to cover some of their expenses.

The result of all this is not only a reduced amount of time available for daily practice, but also a fewer number of years during which relatively concentrated practising is possible, to learn the vast amount of repertoire.

It is all the more important, therefore, to learn how to make the best use of whatever time is available; to develop a more effective way of learning; to establish a carefully thought out plan for daily practising; and to set up a timetable for long-range objectives. It has become more crucial than ever before to acquire a practice technique that will help you to learn better in a shorter time and give you the technical security—and the freedom from worry—to *enjoy* making music.

Even though practising a great many hours daily is not a virtue in itself, nor is it always possible or even necessary, the point of view expressed in this book is not in opposition to a lot of practice: it is specifically and solely against a lot of bad practice, or bad practice habits which cause a lot of wasted time. There are, after all, circumstances in which a great deal of practising may be essential, such as having a deadline for learning new works, preparing a large repertoire for a competition or audition, or substituting at short notice. Still, the longer the practice, the better and more efficient the practice technique should be, so that both the time spent and the result of the practice can be equally more fruitful and enjoyable. Only *good* practice makes perfect.

1 GOOD PRACTISING: THE TEN BASIC RULES

1 Always Know Exactly What You Need to Practise—and Why

There is nothing more frustrating than to spend hours practising without any sign of progress. Therefore, define the problem, spell out the reasons for the difficulty, and devise the correct remedy of practising it.

To practise well, you need to understand the basic principles of violin playing, how to apply them in various ways and how to select the way best suited to your individual physical make-up.

Think what you need to accomplish specifically during the day's practice: three minutes spent thinking about your practising before you start are worth three hours spent in aimless repetition, during which you only learn the bad better.

2 Organise Practice Time to Suit Circumstances

Plan ahead the amount of time you want to spend on each component of your practice material, depending on what you are preparing for and how much time there is available. The plan should include daily, weekly and even longer-range schedules.

There are basically five categories of practising:

1   Learning new material (repertoire and technique).
2   Changing or working on the technical approach to a specific problem (such as vibrato or spiccato).
3   Maintaining and consolidating repertoire and technique.
4   Preparing for a concert, competition or audition.
5   Reviewing old repertoire for any new interpretation.

These categories may combine or overlap but usually one of them is dominant.

Planning a schedule will also be influenced by particular circumstances. You may be:

1   Still in school, subject to a tight class-room timetable.
2   In school and, in addition, working part-time.
3   An amateur with limited time to practise.

4   Already a busy professional.
5   That rare person with unlimited time to practise (on vacation, or just lucky).

Whatever the circumstances, how much should you practise? Generally, no more than is necessary to learn a work so well as to be able to make music without any technical worries. This is the best prescription to banish stage fright. There is no virtue in practising eight hours daily for its own sake: two or three hours of good practice is far better than six hours of bad practice.

It is also important to know yourself, to appraise your strengths and weaknesses objectively, and to adapt your practising technique accordingly. Learn to listen to yourself and to hear yourself objectively.

Some people learn fast and memorize automatically, while others have to learn first how to memorize. Facility of learning may be a mixed blessing: the quick learner may not retain well what he or she has learned, while the one who has to work hard for even the smallest progress may absorb it better and reach a deeper understanding.

3   Repetition is the Mother of Knowledge Only if the Perfected Passage is Repeated More Often than the Faulty One

When you have played a passage or piece for the first time correctly after several unsuccessful attempts, you can feel that the work is done—learned at last! In fact, you have, so far, played the passage incorrectly several times, but correctly only once.

Naturally the incorrect way, having been repeated much more often, will be more readily recalled than the once-played, correct way.

That is why, after having played the passage right for the first time, you must continue to work on it and make sure that it becomes second nature by repeating it *correctly*—bowing and all—until all traces of the faulty ways are erased.

4   Practise Fast as Well as Slowly

Slow practice is essential, in order to allow the brain to encode correctly the various commands it has to send to the muscles for the execution of a given passage, and to judge the correctness of the response and result. But basically, a piece practised slower than its proper tempo is a different piece. The only way to get a true idea of a piece and its problems is to play it in its performance tempo, even in the early stages of learning. The tempo in which a passage has to be played, the speed with which any of the motions has to be executed, are essential and specific elements of the technique involved in its performance.

This has to be taken into account in the very early stages when bowings and fingerings are chosen, otherwise they will not work later. After these bowings and fingerings have been solidified by slow practice, the passage, and the whole piece, have to be practised again in the final tempo in order to learn the appropriate physical motions and mental impulses at their proper speed.

An effective way of practising problematic passages is to combine slow and fast practice, adding the advantage of practising the crucial motions in tempo to the one of having time to think:

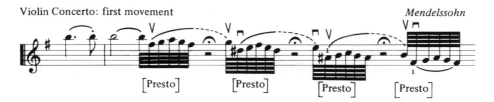

to eliminate the usual gap between bow-changes, or:

to practise the shifts in their proper speed.

The added fermatas provide the time to judge the correctness of the previous passage, to think of the next passage in all its detail, and to formulate the next outgoing command in its entirety.

It is also a good idea to practise fast passages faster than concert tempo (and slow ones slower) in order to build up an extra margin of safety above and beyond the tempo of the performance.

The key to accurate and effortless fast playing is the realization that while the velocity of motion of the fingers and the bow arm increases in faster tempos, the mind should retain a relatively even pace in sending out the commands of execution to the playing mechanism.

In maintaining this even pace in the frequency of commands, however, the brain must increase the amount of information included in every command it sends out at the beginning of each passage. The increased amount of information contained in each command unit is proportionate to the increased tempo, and covers the proportionally greater number of notes to be performed between each command unit. Basically, it works like this:

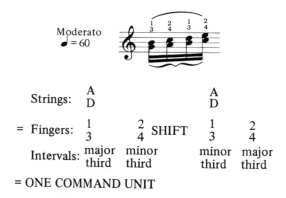

Strings:	A D			A D		
= Fingers:	1 3	2 4	SHIFT	1 3	2 4	
Intervals:	major third	minor third		minor third	major third	

= ONE COMMAND UNIT

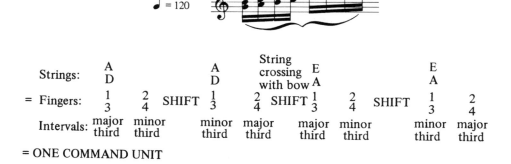

									String crossing with bow	E A			E A	
Strings:	A D			A D											
= Fingers:	1 3	2 4	SHIFT	1 3	2 4	SHIFT	1 3	2 4	SHIFT	1 3	2 4
Intervals:	major third	minor third		minor third	major third		major third	minor third		minor third	major third

= ONE COMMAND UNIT

NOTE: the frequency of command remains at ♩ = 60

In this way the mind will always be in control of the action, instead of running after, or just barely ahead of, the fingers and the bow arm. If the muscles receive orders from the mind belatedly, they react to the emergency in a panicky and jerky manner; the sudden contractions soon degenerate into stiffness and cramps, preventing the fluid, well-prepared and relaxed movements indispensable in fast playing.

In the early stages of practising a work in its ultimate tempo, it will not be possible to play always in tune, or correctly in every way. Keep in mind that the immediate, temporary goal of such practice is to get acquainted with certain problems as they appear only in the final tempo. Purity of intonation, therefore, may be *temporarily* of secondary importance. It is essential, however, that this momentary neglect be corrected as soon as possible, in slow practice.

5   Give Equal Attention to the Bow Arm: Don't Practise Only the Left Hand

The left hand's role constitutes the more obvious activity on a string instrument and its effect is more immediately noticeable as it produces pitch and melody. It is the area, naturally, where most of the practice time tends to be concentrated and where most string players spend 90% of their effort.

But the bow ('the soul of the violin', as the French School claims) and its specific problems should be given just as much attention and practice time in order to perfect all the musical, technical and expressive elements in its domain.

This means not only such basic ingredients of bow technique as détaché, spiccato, and string-crossings: the more subtle elements of the art of bowing are equally important, even if less obvious and more elusive to master.

These include such concerns as choosing the attack and release of a note appropriate to its style and musical character; the nature of bow-change as it is dictated by the demands of phrasing: the various shadings of dynamics; articulation by the bow; accents; experiments in tone colour by various combinations of pressure, speed and distance from the bridge; the speed of the bow as it touches the string in short, off-string notes, thereby determining their style and character; the speed and amount of bow used, and their interaction with left hand and left arm motions; tone quality in general; and, above all, the *expressive capabilities* of the bow.

These aspects of the bow technique are the most difficult to practise because of their less concrete and more aesthetic nature. It is harder to persevere until improvement is noticeable because any change is likely to be gradual and qualitative; the ideal conception must be clear in the mind as a standard against which all progress needs to be measured.

Nevertheless, in the end it is the bow technique, in this more inclusive meaning, which will largely determine the artistic category of a player, and it is the sophisticated use of that technique which, without being obvious, can assist in making a performance extraordinary and memorable.

6   Separate the Problems and Solve Them One by One

Every passage is the sum of many separate and distinct components, each with its own problem. Trying to solve all of them at once will result in improving none of them. Merely repeating a passage as written—and playing it less than correctly—will only grind the mistakes more firmly into the mind.

It is much more productive and time-saving to break down a passage into its components, isolate the problems and concentrate on them separately, and, when corrected, reconstitute and practise them as written.

An example of breaking down a passage into its bow-arm components for practice purposes can be shown in Kreutzer's Study No. 13, as played in the middle of the bow:

(a)   Upper arm motion in crossing strings:

(b)   Fore-arm motion of the détaché:

(c)   Circular hand motion to alternate the détaché between A and D strings:

(d)   Finger action to maintain the bow-hair flat on the strings, counteracting the rolling effect of the hand motion.

Once these component technical elements function well separately, they will combine naturally into one organic, unified motion:

Study No. 13   Kreutzer

This same approach should be used to overcome difficulties in left hand technique. Break down the passage in question into its component elements (including intonation, shifting, sequence of fingers, velocity, articulation) then isolate and practise the problematic passages separately. Only then practise the complete passage as written.

18

7 Practise Difficult Passages in Context

This complements the previous rule.

After having isolated and mastered a specific problem, practise it and ensure that you can play it correctly in the larger context, including the passages immediately preceding and following.

In the following example, the passage of tenths constitute a difficulty which has to be practised at first separately:

Caprice No. 4   *Paganini*

but the jump from the low $b\flat$ immediately preceding it is an important added element for you to consider. Such a rapid displacement greatly influences the disposition of the hand, the arm and all other left-side muscles involved. Added to this, the preceding passage:

involving as it does a quick succession of upward shifts, followed by two sudden and very large jumps in opposite directions, has a crucial bearing on the success of the passage in tenths, and has to be practised eventually together with it. The interaction of neighbouring passages thus emerges as a problem in itself.

Similarly, in practising such passages as this it is not enough to work on the obvious problem of the triad alone:

Violin Concerto No. 4, K.218: first movement   *Mozart*

The initial difficulty for the left hand is getting the first *d″* from nowhere, as it

19

were (the grace note will be automatic). Yet most players only repeat this passage from that first note on, never leaving the 6th position. At the performance, however, one will not have the benefit of a previously established position; one should not have to depend on such elementary devices as plucking the string (which the soloist cannot hear anyway) while the orchestra plays the introduction.

So the first thing to practise and learn securely in this case is finding that first *d″* to rely on during the performance.

Fortunately, due to the shape of a stringed instrument, every single note has its own distinct physical set of characteristics. This is the sum total of such elements as the thickness of the neck and the width of the fingerboard at that particular point, the angle formed by the forearm and upper arm at the left elbow, the distance from the beginning of the fingerboard, the feel of the left hand's palm against the body of the instrument in the higher positions ... and many others.

These can be learned, memorized and relied upon in addition to the conventional method of practising the distance of the shift from a more familiar position (1st or 3rd):

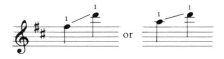

The principle of practising in context extends not only to the technical, but to the musical context as well.

It is one thing to practise the following passage for intonation, important as that is:

Violin Concerto: first movement   *Brahms*

It is quite another to perform it with all the expression and drama it deserves, and which transforms the player's technical approach as well. This results in such changes as a fuller vibrato, greater left-hand finger pressure influencing the intonation (mostly towards sharpness), greater bow-pressure altering tone-production, more body movements, and generally more muscular tension due to the heightened emotional state in a performance.

These reactions should become familiar to the player during practice: the concert is not the time, nor the podium the place, for these manifestations to appear for the first time and to present unknown and disturbing elements.

8 Practise Performing: Don't Only Practise Practising

Practising is not a goal in itself, although it can be very enjoyable. It is only a means by which the real purpose, a technically polished and musically meaningful and exciting performance can be made possible.

But conditions during a performance—both outside and within the performer—are markedly different than those prevailing during practice.

Instead of the familiar surroundings of your own home, the concert hall appears strangely unfamiliar; the comforting knowledge that a mistake can be corrected and a passage repeated without the penalty of anybody's judgment or disapproval (except your own), gives way to the desire to please the audience. Memory, which works well in the solitude of a studio may be distracted by unexpected sights and occurrences during the performance; the different acoustical properties of the hall, and the way in which we perceive them may cause us to play familiar works in an unfamiliar manner; and, most importantly, our own inner reactions to the excitement of the moment, the heightened emotional and muscular tension of an inspired concert performance, in contrast to the relaxed objectivity of a practice run-through, can transform the established premise of the whole playing mechanism.

Ways must be found, therefore, to recreate these performance conditions, and practice time set aside to prepare for them.

After the work on a new piece is well under way, but long before it is finished, attempt a full-scale performance (even unaccompanied) in tempo, and with all musical expression. This will show, before it is too late, what technical and musical changes or improvements need still to be incorporated. During such performance try-outs even try to imagine yourself at the actual concert performance, complete with stage entrance, acknowledging the applause of the audience (which may or may not include several persons known to you), greeting the orchestra when appropriate, and trying to get the 'feeling' of the hall to induce, if possible, the excitement and quickened pulse of the occasion. This in turn can lead to additional technical adjustments or precautions which these physical and psychological circumstances might necessitate. As noted in the previous rule, it is one thing to practise objectively the C minor section of the Brahms Concerto first movement, but quite another to perform it with all the expression and passion. It is yet another matter to do so in the spotlight of unfamiliar surroundings, in front of a full house.

There is also the matter of 'projecting' in a large hall. This has to do with the increased distance between the performer and the audience, and the greater discrepancy between the size of the hall and that of the performer's instrument, both of which reduce the expressive and acoustical impact of the playing.

When a composer *writes* 'piano' or 'forte', that is what he wants to *hear*, but that does not necessarily mean that you have to play merely p or f: the technical means of expression and dynamics have to be intensified, even exaggerated, to counteract the size of the hall; the carrying power of the instrument has to be increased by appropriate tone production, especially when playing with orchestral accompaniment, in order to reach the farthest corners of the auditorium; the conception of the interpretation should be on a par with the dimensions of the hall.

The technical adjustments required must be a part of preparation and basic performance technique, which should not change drastically in a different environment, whether the hall is acoustically 'dead' or 'alive'. Still, it is a good idea to practise from time to time in unfamiliar surroundings and, whenever possible, in the place of the performance itself. Being familiar with the technical and psychological requirements, no matter how unfamiliar the performing circumstances, will create a basis for the security and equilibrium of technique, which is the indispensable pre-requisite of free musical expression.

Lastly, take time to practise in your performing attire. What you wear at the concert can add yet another unfamiliar or restricting element. Ladies should practise in high heels if they are going to wear them at the concert, as such heels throw the body forward, changing its balance and centre of gravity. Men should practise in jacket and tie, not always in shirt-sleeves: the thickness of the lapel and tie between player and instrument can add as much as $\frac{1}{3}''$ (8 mm) to the length of the violin and makes the location of every note that much further away than usual.

9 Practise Also Without the Instrument

Just as the muscles must be trained to practise the physical part of playing, the mind must be exercised separately and independently from the actual playing. It is the brain, after all, which is both the initial and ultimate control centre, and where every action of playing originates.

The human brain has the marvellous capability vividly to recreate past and future occurrences and actions without the actual happenings. This is also true of musical performances. Going through the imaginary performance of a work, complete or in sections, imagining vividly (and correctly) every element connected with its execution (pitch and rhythm, physical motions on the left hand and bow arm, musical expression, and so on) will improve the work of the control centre and, consequently, the actual performance. The computer is only as good as the programming it receives.

This way of practising is not only helpful to the technical aspects of playing, it is especially useful in memorizing. An imaginary performance forces you to know every single note thoroughly as you cannot use the 'prompt' of actually having heard the previous note, nor be 'prompted' into playing the next note or passage by the physical impetus of having just played the previous one. That means that as much pertinent information about the note, and as many of its characteristics as possible, must be firmly fixed in the mind.

If you can play through a work mentally, in tempo and without any lapses or hesitations (judging yourself honestly), you can safely say that the work is completely and securely memorized. Otherwise the weak spots will show up: there will be an inevitable breakdown in recall at the critical moments.

I discovered the usefulness of this kind of practice for myself purely by accident and as a result of dire necessity. Living in Paris in the aftermath of World War II, awaiting my overdue American visa in miserable circumstances, I had some concerts to play but the room where I was staying had no heat or running water. The winter was so cold that I had to stay in bed most of the day to keep warm. Still in bed, but wanting to practise, I started to play through my repertoire in my mind. I soon found that, mentally, I could go through those pieces really well without music, practise and improve the trouble spots just by reading the music (propped up on the bedspread), and later learn whole new pieces, still without the instrument. When it finally came to the performances, they went without a hitch.

A few years later, the soundness of this method of practising, developed to the point where a certain imaginary action will produce a *practical* result, was confirmed by Georges Enesco. One day, driving with Paul Rolland, Enesco took a pencil out of his pocket and started to move his left hand fingers on it as if it were the neck of the violin. I watched as he continued to 'practise', until he stopped abruptly and, looking at me, said, "Oops! That was out of tune".

Such mental and silent practice is also ideal to establish initial bowings and fingerings for a new piece. With experience you will find that few of them will have to be changed in the actual playing.

Mental practising also offers a way to work when you are physically tired or ill, and is often the only way to practise as you are travelling to, or just before, a concert.

To hear the music in the inner ear is essential to mental practising. Inner hearing should be developed by every musician, but it is a *must* for those who have an instrument on which you have to create the pitch of every note (and for singers, conductors . . . and composers).

10   Do Not Neglect the 'Easy' Sections: They Tend to Take Revenge on You!

Most music contains passages which pose no problems even at first reading. The usual tendency is, consequently, to neglect these passages completely in practising.

It is true that you need not spend as much practice time on the easy as on the difficult passages. But unless they receive a certain minimum amount of attention (which should be considerably more than nothing), those 'easy' sections will be blank spots in your mind amidst all the other, well-practised passages. At the performance they can appear totally unfamiliar, as if one had never played them at all.

This unfamiliarity might cause just that momentary hesitation. "Is this right?" "What finger do I play this note with?" "Do I shift here or later?" Many an otherwise well-learned piece can break down at such a moment. (A momentary psychological let down can occur at any time, but it often occurs near the end of a piece as you relax with the end in sight.)

2 FINGER-PATTERN PRACTICE I: THE NEW TABLATURE

Keyboard players have the advantage over string players not only because of the 'ready-made' nature of the keyboard, with its fixed and pre-arranged pitches, but also by the fact that the whole range of the piano, every note they have to play, is in front of them visually as well. From this tangible and permanent framework they can readily identify and select any note they need to play. String players, on the other hand, not only have to create their own pitch for every note, even while holding or balancing their instrument, but have to do so on an unmarked fingerboard without any visual aid.

To adapt the advantages of the keyboard and to apply them to string playing, the New Tablature establishes a system which combines a visual representation of the fingerboard with the systematic organization of virtually all of the possible note-combinations on the fingerboard. The term 'Tablature' is used to describe many European and Asian systems of notation which tell the reader directly where to place each finger on a string fingerboard or keyboard. Such systems were much used in the early days of printed music for lute, bowed strings and keyboard instruments in the 16th and 17th century. An early example is Hans Gerle's *Musica Teusch* for lute and bowed strings printed in Nuremberg in 1532. The directions not only told the reader exactly where to play every given note but also gave rhythm symbols to show the length of every given note and so provided all the indications necessary for performing the music. The modern tablature borrows only the indication of pitch directly and is designed specifically to help practising.

This new concept, which is in effect a new way of thinking about left-hand technique, rests on a double foundation:

(1) A 'Gridiron' of the fingerboard (the counterpart of the piano keyboard).
(2) A 'Finger-Pattern' system (the comprehensive organization and classification of the *infinite* number of note-combinations into a *limited* number of readily identifiable, recurring patterns).

The Gridiron of the Fingerboard

The complete range of the violin is about $4\frac{1}{2}$ octaves, or 54 semitones:

25

The range of each of the four strings, for practical purposes, is about two octaves, or 25 semitones:

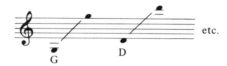

This means that there are at least 100 different spaces on the fingerboard in which to play the 54 semitones (since many notes are playable at more than one place). These 100 or so spaces, like the 88 keys of the piano, can serve as a simple but effective and permanent mental-visual framework, dividing the fingerboard into a gridiron of 4 × 25 squares.

It will be appreciated that, in the schematic illustration opposite, strings are represented as a succession of rectangles instead of lines; and that the ratios of the fingerboard and diminution of spaces (intervals) in the higher position are approximate.

On such a fingerboard every note has its own permanent and pre-arranged slot, giving the player a mental guidance system in which not only the target of the fingers, but the relative distances and the relationships between the fingers can be instantly and positively identified and visualized. The classification and condensation of all note and finger combinations into a few basic and recurring finger patterns will enable you to think and play in larger units, or groups of notes, instead of single notes. You can learn to recognize and read notes as words or paragraphs instead of single letters. When this system of patterns is superimposed on the keyboard-gridiron of the fingerboard, you will have a complete guidance system to improve the left-hand speed, accuracy and intonation. You will take 'guesswork' out of string playing.

FINGERBOARD

G	D	A	E
A♭	E♭	B♭	F
A	E	B	F#
B♭	F	C	G
B	F#	C#	G#
C	G	D	A
D♭	A♭	E♭	B♭
D	A	E	B
E♭	B♭	F	C
E	B	F#	C#
F	C	G	D
G♭	D♭	A♭	E♭
G	D	A	E
A♭	E♭	B♭	F
A	E	B	F#
B♭	F	C	G
B	F#	C#	G#
C	G	D	A
D♭	A♭	E♭	B♭
D	A	E	B
E♭	B♭	F	C
E	B	F#	C#
F	C	G	D
G♭	D♭	A♭	E♭
G	D	A	E
			F
			F#
			G
			G#
			A
			B♭
			B
			C

BRIDGE

The Comprehensive System of Finger-Patterns

The combinations and permutations of notes and fingers which are possible on the violin, or on any string instrument, amount to an astronomical figure. Not only can the 54 different semitones be played in 100 or more different spaces, but most of the notes can be played with any of the four fingers.

If you add groups of notes or whole passages, chords and double stops as well, the sum total of all these variations and combinations is truly staggering. However, there are only a limited number of combinations into which the four playing fingers can be arranged to perform the limitless number of passages and groups of notes. Organized systematically, the whole range of violin and viola literature can be traced and identified as belonging, at any given time, to one or another of this limited number of finger combinations. These in turn are determined by a momentary disposition of the fingers: the pattern of whole-steps and half steps between them. The number of different patterns is limited by the diatonic-chromatic nature of most Western music, and by the normal range between the 1st and 4th finger on one string: a fourth.

The first four notes of the major scale, starting with the first finger, give:

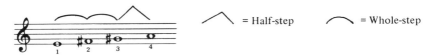

To visualize this pattern, and to judge better the prevailing distances and relationships between the fingers, here it is placed on the framework of the fingerboard 'gridiron':

Pattern No. 1:

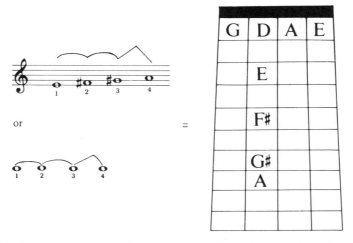

or   =

(Unoccupied spaces are no longer 'named' and these locations should be memorized.)

28

Starting the major scale on the 2nd, 3rd and 4th note respectively, with the first finger, in any key, on any string and in any position, gives:

Pattern No. 2

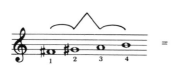

G	D	A	E
	F♯		
	G♯		
	A		
	B		

Pattern No. 3

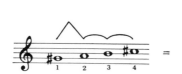

G	D	A	E
	G♯		
	A		
	B		
	C♯		

Pattern No. 4

=

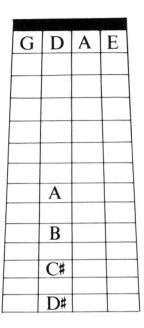

These four basic patterns, which are the most common finger-combinations in violin and viola literature, have been used in their most elementary and embryonic forms in some violin 'methods' for beginners. With the New Tablature, the concept of patterns is expanded and built into a comprehensive organisation, encompassing the whole fingerboard with virtually every possible combination of notes, fingers, strings and positions.

In following the system, you need to recognize 12 points:

(1)   A pattern remains the same whether all the fingers are on one string or are distributed on several strings: the whole-step, half-step relationship between the fingers is only minimally influenced by the differential of the space between strings:

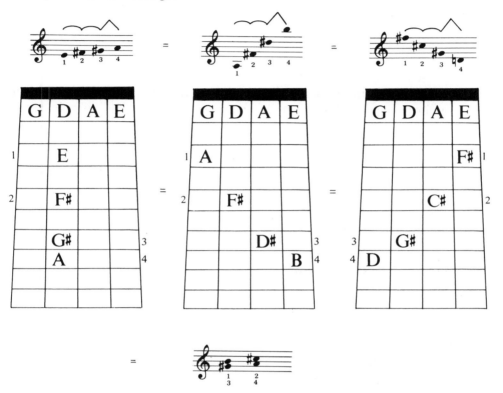

(2)   A pattern remains the same in any position along the fingerboard, taking into account the gradually smaller intervals in higher positions:

(3)   A pattern of a separate category can be established, added to the group of diatonic patterns, in which distances between fingers can be greater than a whole-step, making step-and-a-half and even two steps:

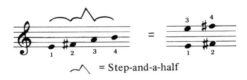

(4)   A pattern remains the same whether the notes are played consecutively or simultaneously as in chords or double-stops:

32

(5) A pattern is interchangeable in its sequence of fingers:

(6) A pattern is still recognizable, though incomplete, even if only three fingers are involved. For example, this can be seen as Pattern No. 4:

Partita in D minor:
Chaconne   *J. S. Bach*

(7) A pattern can be made up of any combination of fingers and strings; as in this example of Pattern No. 3:

(8) A pattern may be followed by several different patterns to make up one long passage:

Sonata in D, op.94a: Scherzo   *Prokofiev*

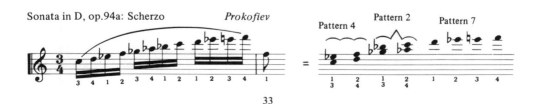

33

(9) A pattern may contain chords (as in Baroque practice) divided into arpeggio:

or double-stops reduced to consecutive single notes:

Pattern 4

(10) A pattern is easily recognized, if all fingers are on the same string, by noting the intervals between the fingers:

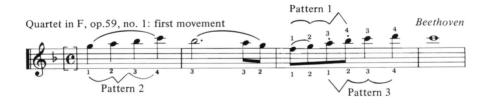

(11) A pattern in which the fingers are on more than one string can be transferred to a single string by adding a connecting perfect 5th up or down (as shown by arrows here):

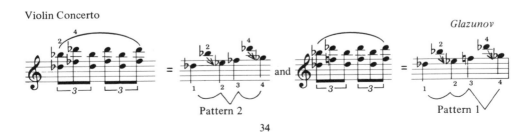

(12)   Whatever the pattern, for the sake of good intonation choosing higher fingers on higher strings may form a more natural hand position:

and higher fingers on lower strings with an inward turn of the palm a more strenuous position:

The Complete System will be found on pages 89 to 96.

3 FINGER-PATTERN PRACTICE II: GOOD INTONATION

The elusive goal of 'perfect' intonation is almost impossible to achieve on a stringed instrument. It is like trying to hit the bulls-eye of a small, moving target every time with a bow and arrow, from a bicycle on a tightrope. The term itself is a subjective definition, due to several conflicting elements which determine pitch in our tonal system. Nevertheless, the importance of excellent intonation can hardly be over-emphasized. While an exciting, inspired and brilliant performance makes the listener forgive a momentary lapse in intonation, there is no question that several lapses even minimal, detract from the overall effect and linger unpleasantly in the memory.

Pythagoras demonstrated that 12 theoretically or mathematically perfect fifths, placed on top of each other, do not equal 7 perfect octaves as they should, but result in a difference of pitch (the Pythagorean 'comma'). The same is true of three major thirds or four minor thirds which, put on top of each other, should but do not equal a perfect octave:

Major thirds   Minor thirds   do not add up to

The 'well-tempered' tuning of a keyboard instrument (the string player's usual companion in performance) results in distributing this Pythagorean difference in pitch equally along the keyboard. The natural tendency of string players (or any players of instruments with changeable pitch) is to differentiate between a '$d\#$' and an '$e\flat$', for example, depending on the musical context, in what might be called 'characteristic' or 'functional' intonation. Leading tones are slightly sharp, flats are lower than their enharmonic counterparts and so on, obeying the harmonic function and melodic direction of the notes for the sake of what Roger Sessions calls 'purer' intonation.

Perfect intonation is therefore not an absolute or immobile conception. 'Good' intonation must necessarily be the result of compromise within very narrow limits, according to the prevalent key and harmonic structure of the piece. It has to conform to the 'ensemble' of every note within a single instrument and must relate to every other instrument in an ensemble. A note is 'in tune' if its melodic, harmonic and expressive function is clear and in accord with all other notes, harmonies and chordal structures of the work as a whole.

Good intonation also depends on being able to hear the pitch of a coming note in advance and on a vivid preconception of the actual physical sensation of playing that note—its location, distance, direction and 'feel'—in relation to those you are already playing. The physical approach to the instrument and the playing mechanism itself must be natural if you are to do this effortlessly. Too much muscular tension, for instance, causes the ear-drum to tighten and prevents the ear from registering the sound waves fully or objectively. The human ear is a very adaptable organ, but it is mainly a measuring instrument like a metronome (but measuring pitch and dynamics as well as time): neither makes a quality judgment by itself. This is imposed by the brain in accordance with pre-set standards of pitch and dynamics. Incorruptibly high *mental* standards of intonation must be guarded unceasingly and be compared—as measured by the ear—with every succession of notes.

The tablature system provides an accurate framework for good intonation, first of all by assigning a specific 'slot' to each note on the fingerboard and visualizing it, then by organizing the slots into a limited number of patterns. These patterns establish the relationships and distances between the left-hand fingers both along and across the fingerboard in any one location; and in doing this, they help to identify the exact location of every note visually, mentally and physically before the actual sound is played.

Fortunately for the sake of identification and accuracy, every note on a stringed instrument is physically different, however slightly, from every other note because:

(1) The fingerboard 'flares out' toward the higher positions.
(2) The neck widens and deepens toward the body of the instrument.
(3) The distance between similar intervals reduces in higher positions.
(4) The main body of the instrument is physically felt from the 3rd or 4th position upwards.
(5) The height of strings and their spacing above the fingerboard both increase toward the bridge.
(6) The four strings are of different thicknesses.
(7) The strings are at various distances from the palm of the left hand.
(8) The distance of each note from the nut or bridge differs according to the various angles formed between the forearm and the upper arm, the upper arm and the player's body . . . and the bent wrist.
(9) Distance can also be judged from the head or the face of the player.
(10) The rotation of the left arm differs.

Every note is the sum of these physical characteristics and distinguished from every other note to the extent that the characteristics vary. These subtle variations must be noticed and knowledge of them practised—in addition to the obvious differences of pitch, duration, dynamics and tone quality—before you can accurately project, and unerringly find, every note on the fingerboard.

If the importance of good intonation is self-evident in the traditional literature, it is no less important in contemporary and avant-garde works—at least in those that are based on *some* tonal system—where true 'functional' intonation may be essential to the understanding and appreciation of the work. Out-of-tune playing in well-known repertoire works, or in those where the traditional melodic and harmonic structure is familiar, will merely expose the poor intonation of the performer. Playing inaccurately and out-of-tune in a new contemporary work, on the other hand, may reduce it to a confused and senseless noise which can unjustly condemn it . . . and its composer, who deserves a fair hearing. The performer has the responsibility both toward himself and toward the composer whose work he is performing.

4 FINGER-PATTERN PRACTICE III: INTONATION EXERCISES

Here are suggested exercises based on each of the four basic finger patterns, to which you can add your own. Examples from the standard repertory show how these exercises translate into passages for performance: learn to re-translate such passages back into their patterns for practice. Extra technical suggestions to apply to these exercises follow at the end of the chapter.

PATTERN NO. 1:

Higher fingers on higher strings:

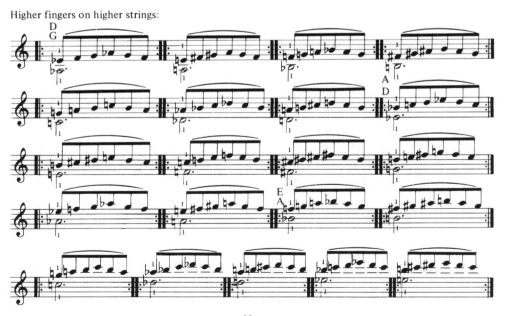

Higher fingers on lower strings (palm rotated towards the neck):

Various additional combinations:

*Add your
own inventions*

Practise each example up-scale in semi-tones

For independence of fingers:

*Repeat
up-scale in
semi-tones*

Double-stops and Tremolos:

Practise very slowly at first

Fourths and Sixths:

40

On 3 strings:

On 4 strings:

Arpeggios:

NOTE:
Pattern 1 can still be recognised when only three fingers are used:

PATTERN NO. 1: EXAMPLES FROM THE REPERTORY

Sonata No. 1: Fuga

Bach

Partita No. 3: Bourrée

Bach

PATTERN NO. 2:

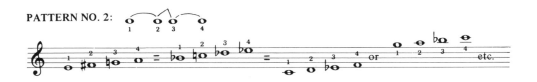

Higher fingers on higher strings:

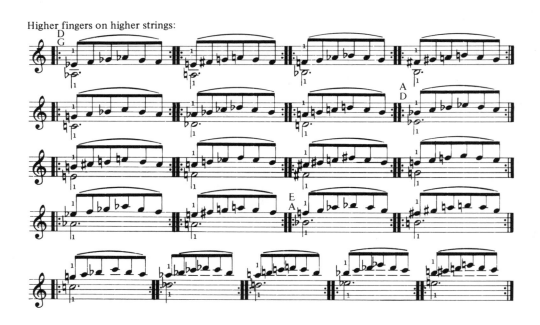

Higher fingers on lower strings:

Various additional combinations:

Repeat up-scale in semi-tones

For independence of fingers:

Repeat up-scale in semi-tones

Double stops and tremolos

Fourths and Sixths:

On 3 strings:

On 4 strings:

Arpeggios

NOTE:
Pattern 2 can still be recognised when only three fingers are used:

PATTERN NO. 2: EXAMPLES FROM THE REPERTORY

Candenza for Mozart Violin Concerto No. 4   *Joachim*

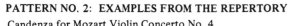

Cadenza from the Violin Concerto   *Mendelssohn*

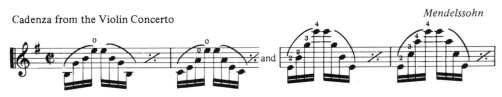

Violin Concerto　　　　　　　　　　*Delius*

Violin Concerto No. 2: third movement　　　　　　　*Bartok*

PATTERN NO. 3:

Higher fingers on higher strings:

Higher fingers on lower strings:

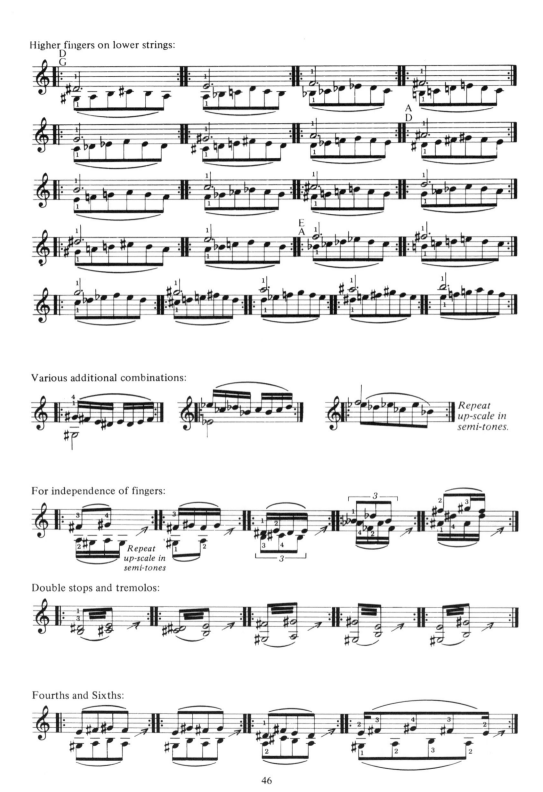

Various additional combinations:

Repeat up-scale in semi-tones.

For independence of fingers:

Repeat up-scale in semi-tones

Double stops and tremolos:

Fourths and Sixths:

46

On 3 strings:

On 4 strings:

Arpeggios:

NOTE:
Pattern 3 can still be recognised when only three fingers are used:

PATTERN NO. 3: **EXAMPLES FROM THE REPERTORY**

Moto Perpetuo   *Paganini*

47

Sonata No. 3: Fuga

and

Bach

PATTERN NO. 4:

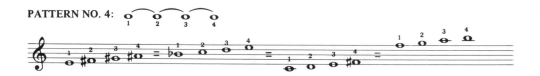

Higher fingers on higher strings:

Higher fingers on lower strings:

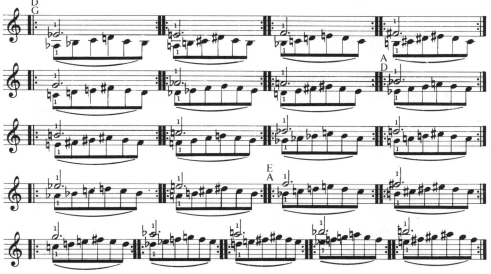

Various additional combinations:

Repeat up-scale in semi-tones

For independence of fingers:

Repeat up-scale in semi-tones

Double stops and tremolos:

Fourths and Sixths:

On 3 strings:

On 4 strings:

'Geminiani' chord

etc.

(for 'correct' hand position)

Arpeggios:

NOTE:
Pattern 4 can still be recognised when only three fingers are used:

PATTERN NO. 4: EXAMPLES FROM THE REPERTORY

Violin Concerto   *Glazunov*

Sonata No. 6   *8ve*   *Ysaÿe*

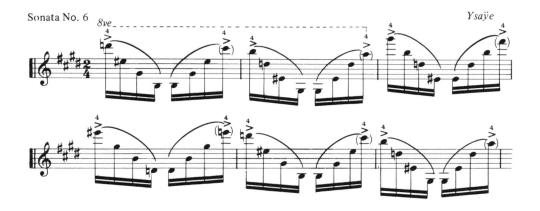

(1)   Practice these exercises *very* slowly at first. Listen intensely and try to come as close to perfect intonation as possible. It might appear at first that your intonation is getting worse, when in reality it is your hearing that is getting better and more acute, more sensitive to the slightest deviation from the 'true' pitch.

(2)   When you proceed up-scale chromatically, start from the lowest notes on the G and D strings, until you reach the 4th or 5th position, then start again the same way on the D and A strings and finally on the A and E strings. Notice, practise and memorize the distance and feel of the half-steps and the rate at which the space of this same interval diminishes in the higher positions. Later, move up-scale diatonically and eventually by even larger 'skips'. Finally, change the routine: mix patterns, starting in high position and proceeding down-scale, for example.

(3)   Make sure that your hand-position is natural and comfortable, so that you can play every combination in a given pattern without any major adjustment of the left hand. The only noticeable difference in the hand-position of the same pattern should be the result of a change in the basic distribution of the fingers on the various strings: higher fingers on higher strings, or higher fingers on lower strings and vice versa. This difference will be reflected in the various degrees of left-arm rotation and in turning the left-hand palm toward, or away from, the neck of the violin.

(4)   When correcting the pitch, move the fingertip, do not merely twist the finger or change its angle or direction only. Corrections should be made without changing the bow, which should be drawn slowly and steadily. When you are satisfied with the pitch, memorize the feeling of the exact location and position of the hand, arm and fingers for that particular note or group of notes for future recall. For pitch control and comparison, most of these exercises are in double stops: for example the initial exercises in each basic pattern sustain the perfect fifth with the first finger. Later combinations involve broken chords and arpeggios.

(5) Invent your own combinations and exercises based on these examples, at first within the same pattern, later in mixed patterns. One of the most important aspects of these exercises is that you can fashion them to your individual needs. Those shown here should serve as examples and are intended to stimulate your own imagination. Practise most those combinations or patterns which give you the most problems.

(6) Select difficult passages from the repertoire, reduce them to the underlying pattern and add the resulting combinations to these exercises. As an example, here is a passage reduced to its basic pattern for practice:

Violin Concerto: first movement   *Brahms*

Pattern: Intervals on one string:

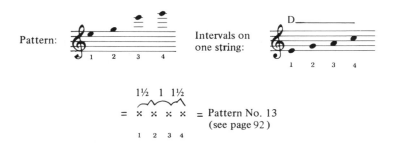

To practise, play:

then:

52

(7)   Practise these exercises without vibrato at first, but maintaining a relaxed readiness to vibrate at any moment. Too much vibrato, or too wide a vibrato, especially in higher positions, tends to obscure the intonation and cover up imperfections, making it harder to hear and correct them. When you do, later, use vibrato, remember that the extent of its range is from slightly below the pitch and *up to* the pitch but *not above* it. The upward pulsations created by the motion of the vibrato should reinforce the pitch itself in the ear, not anything higher, which would make the note appear sharp.

Until the pattern system becomes familiar, you will need about 15–20 minutes daily practice; after that, 5–10 minutes should be enough, choosing one or two patterns daily and a few exercises from each pattern. The same method, including *your own* exercises, should then be followed in any of the other, less prevalent, patterns shown in the table on pages 90–93.

5 LEFT HAND PRACTICE

Any guidance on the choice of fingering for practising must be dependent to a large extent on your physical make-up. The instrument should be fitted to the player, not the other way around. Specifically, characteristics to be considered are: size of hand; length and thickness of fingers; shape of shoulders; length of arms; and 'length' of neck. These characteristics may call for the use of a shoulder pad or even for a closer spacing of strings by cutting new grooves at the nut or at the bridge of the violin. The following guidelines will help you to feel 'at home' with the instrument:

(1)   Contracted fingerings (a) suit small hands; extended fingerings (b) suit large hands:

To prevent muscle stiffness, leading to poor intonation, small hands should avoid strenuous stretches while large hands must beware cramped fingers.

(2)   For clean and unnoticeable changes of position (technical shifts), choose where possible:

(a) a shift at the change of the bow,
(b) a shift with the rhythm—on the beat,
(c) a shift on the half-step instead of a whole-step when the shift has to be made with the same finger.

(3)   Make one large shift, rather than two small, in fast passages. Sudden or too frequent changes of position prevent the hand from settling in any one position. This affects adversely the accuracy of the shift and, consequently, its intonation. Here (a) is better than (b):

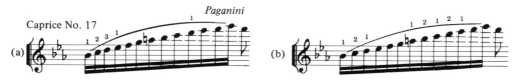

(4)   Upward shifts = up-bow; downward shifts = down-bow. It is not natural for the human body to move arms or legs in parallel motion. So on the violin, the two arms move best mirror-wise, either away from, or toward each other. This maintains a much better body balance than if the two arms are moving in the same direction.

(5)   In practising scales, do not always start on the lowest note. Start, for instance, on the top note, go down, then up again to finish on the top note. Begin on any other note of the scale, shifting the natural accents and alternating them among all the notes to make them rhythmically even. It is also sometimes useful to play scales with the 3rd and 4th finger only to strengthen the 4th finger:

Occasionally, fast scale practice is also important to learn the sequence, order and succession of the combined finger motions, shifts, string crossings and bow changes: the 'programming' or 'computerising' of larger units, or groups of notes. It is also helpful to divide scales into two halves and practise the two different sets of problems they represent separately (three- and four-octave scales). Play the lower section in one position but across the strings, and the upper section from the first note on the E string to the top, on the same string but in different positions:

(6)   Practise shifts in double-stops where the shift involves a change of string. In the following, for example, the first finger b' is placed on the A string and the third finger a'' on the E string, as a double-stop:

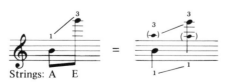

55

When you make the shift, you will then connect *positions* instead of *single notes*—a much more secure procedure.

(7)   For smooth, clean string crossings in rapid passages practise with both fingers down on the two neighbouring strings, in double stops:

This way the bow will not have to wait or hesitate, or get to the next string ahead of the left hand finger.

(8)   Pay particular attention to down-scale legato passages. Note that it is easier to achieve clear articulation, evenness and sharp rhythm with the left hand in up-scale passages, when the fingers can be put on the string with a more or less snappy click, than down-scale when the fingers are merely lifted off the string, in a 'negative' finger action. To counterbalance this, cellists often use a motion akin to left-hand pizzicato. This can also be used, judiciously, in violin or viola playing.

(9)   Treat the hand and the arm as a unit in which the arm, with its larger muscles, has the task of moving the hand over the spot from which the finger(s) can be placed accurately on pitch, reserving the smaller muscles for the more delicate precision tasks.

6 BOWING PRACTICE

In violin playing, as in the playing of any other musical instrument, there are certain rules of common sense arising from the nature of the instrument which, because they are so self-evident, tend to be overlooked or forgotten. While all such rule-of-thumb guidelines have their exceptions, observe the following whenever possible—and where there are no compelling reasons to the contrary—to develop a more natural, efficient and expressive bow technique.

1 Down-Bow for Down-Beat; Up-Bow for Up-Beat

Started near or at the frog, the down-bow benefits from the pull of gravity in the same direction, from the added weight of the frog end of the bow and from the more direct and immediate transmission of that weight by both the arm and hand in the vicinity of the frog. It is therefore more naturally suited to express the emphatic character of a heavy beat, as the up-bow is to a light beat. But remember:

(1)   Do not start every down-bow at the frog (or even necessarily in the lower half) nor every up-bow at the tip. This is a fairly common mistake when following bowing marks in letter only, not in spirit. The *required amount* of bow, as determined by the number and length of notes to be played, with what dynamics and at what tempo, should dictate the place on the bow where a specific up-bow or down-bow should begin.

(2)   If the upbeat consists of one bow stroke (or an uneven number of strokes) start up-bow, so the down-beat can fall on a down bow.

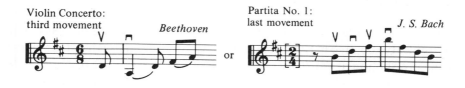

If it consists of two or any *even* number of strokes, start down bow, preferably in the upper half, to preserve the 'light' character of the up-beat.

(3)   Common sense may provide more comfortable exceptions. In (a) of the following the long and continuous détaché passage of semiquavers (or 16th-notes) follows more naturally a 'down-up' beginning. In (b) and (c) the down-beat is played 'up-bow' because it is more natural to land *on* the string (and easier to remain there without re-bounding) in 'down-bow' for the longer, on-string strokes which follow the short, off-string notes. Take care, however, to accentuate the heavy note of the down-beat as marked— and not the first note of the next 'down-bow'.

2   Equal Bow-Length for Equal Note-Values

This is a basic rule of good 'bowmanship', as any change in bow speed will cause a noticeable change in dynamics and accentuation unless the other elements of tone production are also changed at the same time. Failure to observe this rule accounts for much faulty phrasing, unwanted and unmusical accents, and unplanned diminuendos toward the tip. It can also be the cause of poor ensemble playing in chamber and orchestral music: a string section which merely follows the same *direction* of the bow will not sound unified, or even together, unless everyone uses the same *amount* and the same *part* of the bow.

While the length of the bow available is the same in the up-bow or down-bow, the length of notes or phrases during each stroke is not necessarily so and the use of the bow should reflect this variety. Here is a good example of the need to distribute the bow carefully:

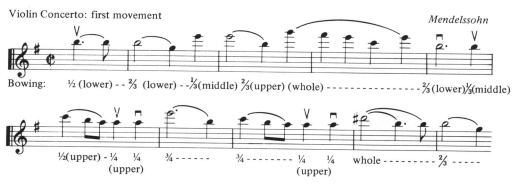

Violin Concerto: first movement

Mendelssohn

Bowing: ½ (lower) - - ⅔ (lower) - -⅓(middle) ⅔(upper) (whole) - - - - - - - - - - - - - - - - ⅔ (lower)⅓(middle)

½(upper) - ¼   ¼   ¾ - - - - - -   ¾ - - - - - - - - ¼   ¼   whole - - - - - - - - ⅔ - - - - -
         (upper)   (upper)

Although these fractions of bow-length must be approximate, and bow-speed and pressure still have to be slightly adjusted to the contour of the phrase, observing these divisions and the principle behind them will make it much easier to come closer to the ideal musical expression of this lovely and so often mis-played passage.

3   Down-Bow for Up-Scales; Up-Bow for Down-Scales

There are several advantages in this bowing, crossing from lower to higher—and higher to lower—strings:

(1)   Clockwise movement is more natural for the bow arm in the down-bow . . . and vice versa.

(2)   The arm follows the curvature of the bridge.

(3)   The bow seems 'longer', actually gaining the distance between two strings with each string crossing, whereas it loses the same length if you move in the opposite direction:

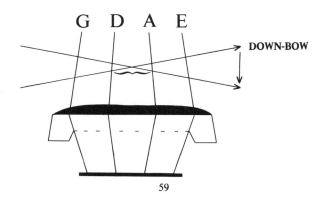

4   Phrasing Marks are not always Bowing Marks

To choose the most appropriate bowings, try to look at a facsimile or unedited Urtext of a work, and keep in mind that most composers indicate phrasings and *not* bowings in their music. Very often their ideal slurs or ties indicating a phrase or articulation cannot be followed literally in performance as bowings. When they have to be divided or changed for any reason, try always to remain faithful to the composer's intentions as expressed in his phrasing or articulation marks...yet there can be reasons for changing the original indications. Large halls (or outdoors) may need more sound. A technically difficult, or musically problematic passage may sound better with a sharper rhythmical definition. Whatever the reason for the change, the sound should convey the original ideas of the composer, even if the bowings you choose to carry out those ideas are different from the original phrasing marks.

The markings in Bach, Handel and many 18th-century works represent a very special case. Most composers of that time played and knew the instrument very well and carefully marked solo pieces in particular with indications valid and practical not only as phrasings, but also as bowings. It is *indispensable* to have the Urtext of such works at hand at your practice, and alterations should be made only for good reasons, such as finding a similar passage elsewhere which appears to have more appropriate or applicable markings. (Even Bach and Handel were not *always* consistent.)

5   Complex String Crossings are Clearer Without Left-Hand Notes

String crossings often involve a series of complicated bow-arm motions, and it is very important to have a clear idea of the combined pattern they form. So reduce the passage to its bowing essentials by playing the open strings in identical sequence and duration without the left hand like this:

Photographic experiments with a small light bulb attached to the frog-end of the bow show that in playing example (a) the light describes a 'figure 8', more or less elongated according to the amount of bow used. Being able to visualize patterns like this, like finger patterns, helps greatly in learning correct bow movements which then fall automatically into place when put together with the left hand. Basic rule no. 6 (see page 17) applies here as much as anywhere: concentrate on one problem at a time.

6   The Faster the Bow, the Shorter the Arm Used

This is the rule of the pendulum: an object swinging between two extremities moves at a speed dependent on its distance from the hanging point. The whole bowing-arm is a 'three-in-one' pendulum of upper-arm, forearm and hand. It is also an adjustable pendulum: the whole arm is the longest and slowest, hanging from the shoulder; the hand is the shortest and fastest, hanging from the wrist; and the forearm and hand used together are in between the two, hanging from the elbow. The righthand fingers take no part in the pendulum but *react* like shock absorbers.

An efficient and relaxed bow technique can be achieved by using the length of bow in inverse proportion to its speed. The speed of the bow also determines the section of bow to be used:

(1)   The faster the bow, the shorter the arm, the lesser the bow and towards the tip.
(2)   The slower the bow, the longer the arm, the greater the bow and towards the frog.

These rules may be modified by dynamic or tonal considerations but they remain the basis for all good bowing. A good spiccato in particular, at any speed, depends essentially on 'the pendulum rule'.

7   More Bow Rather Than More Pressure

Long, fast bows give a greater freedom and physical well-being in performance. In proportion to pressure (which at the point of contact contributes to the tone quality), a long, fast bow contributes more to a large, pure tone of great carrying power. Too much sustained pressure in a slow bow will lead to stiffness and, because the pressure often tends to be exerted by the small finger muscles, the whole bowing arm becomes taut and leads to a forced tone. Where you have the choice use more bow rather than more pressure.

8   Avoid Crossing Strings for a Single Note in Fast Passages

In fast passages there is often a choice between using an open string or the fourth finger. As a rule, avoid crossing strings for a single note in a passage otherwise on the same string, like this:

Yet continued uniformity of bowing may take preference over more difficult fingering. Here the upper fingering needs a sudden shift, whereas the lower fingering needs a complex mixture of bowing:

As you continue to plan your practising, you will always have to decide whether to concentrate on bowing or fingering in any passage (difficult or easy). Always concentrate on the greater difficulty. The choice is yours . . .but realise that it is a choice to be made *before* you practise one too much in preference to the other.

7 SIGHTREADING PRACTICE I: FIRST STEPS

Sightreading is the ability to perform a work of music, not previously played by the performer, at first sight, and as accurately as possible. To read a piece accurately, the player needs to observe, in addition to correct pitch and rhythm, all the dynamic and expressive marks in a way that demonstrates a general understanding of the composition's musical meaning. While this may appear to be an impressive feat—and, indeed, it is—proficiency in sightreading should be the logical result of a musician's training, the sum of musicianship and technical knowledge of the instrument, and a proof of competence as a performer. Once the mental and physical activity of sightreading is put in its proper perspective, the task will no longer seem so formidable: a large number of the problems in sightreading stem from not understanding, and therefore overestimating, the difficulties.

In our everyday life we sightread constantly: whenever we glance at a newspaper, or read a 'flash' TV advertisement, we read that particular text for the first time, 'at first sight'. That is to say, we read that text for the first time *as a whole*, not in its basic components. These components are already familiar to us from previous experiences, and what enables us to understand such texts instantly is the fact that in Western languages we already know the alphabet and the grammar, and more than likely we have encountered previously and recognize most of the individual words which make up the text in question. It is the particular combination of words and correlation of their meaning in a new context which is novel and constitutes reading 'at first sight'. If we take for granted our ability in reading out loud to understand written symbols, translate them into concepts, thoughts and ideas, and transform them instantly and automatically into spoken words ('perform' them)—sometimes in several languages—why can't we expect the same skill in music?

When the elements of technique and musicianship—the basic musical 'alphabet' and 'grammar'—have been learned, and all scales, arpeggios, finger-patterns and ways of bowing have been assimilated, virtually no musical text has to be read or played, strictly speaking, at first sight any longer. By then, at one time or another, in one place or another, you will have played with basic building blocks of instrumental technique and musicianship which make up the various individual compositions in most musical styles.

Sightreading, then, is simply the ability to recognize from previous experience the basic and familiar technical and musical components, the mental capacity to recombine them as they appear in a given piece, and the technical skill to perform them instantly on the instrument in their new combinations. Looked at from this perspective, sightreading, just like any other phase of instrumental technique, can become easier by judicious and intelligent practice, which is designed to develop and perfect it.

The literature of classical music is full of works built almost entirely from the simplest musical elements of scales, broken thirds and triads, and arpeggios. One example will be sufficient to illustrate it:

Violin Concerto: first movement *Beethoven*

ibid: first movement *ibid:* third movement

This demonstrates once again the importance and great value of practising—and *memorizing*—scales, arpeggios, broken thirds, octaves, and so on. A work like the Scale System of Carl Flesch, for example, is a complete grammar of the language of classical violin music. Memorizing, it will be apparent, is important not only to perform without music, but also to recognize and recall the memorized elements when sightreading them in a new context.

Since facts which are clearly organized into a system are also easier for the brain to memorize, knowledge of the finger-patterns and the table of shifts, combined with the visual aid of the tablature and the systematic study of the various bowings, will make all these mental, technical and musical building blocks easily recalled. They are then available to transform the written notes into sound, the context into live music.

Another factor which helps fluent sightreading is familiarity with a composer's style. Many composers—and groups of composers—may be recognizable through features of harmonic and melodic vocabulary, modulation, turns of phrase, cadences, rhythms; they have their musical manner of speaking and writing. When you can recognize these characteristics, you can to a certain extent 'read ahead' and, without looking at every note, have a good idea of what is coming next. This is especially true in the musical language of the period of tonality, but even some of today's avant-garde composers have a recognizable language of their own, often associated with a recurring visual image in their notation.

The idea of a composer's recognizable individuality is beautifully expressed by Eduard Hanslick, the noted 19th-century Viennese critic, in his account of the very first performance, in 1865, of Schubert's long lost 'Unfinished' Symphony:

> When, after the few introductory measures, clarinet and oboe in unison began their gentle cantilena above the calm murmur of the violins, every child recognized the composer, and a muffled "Schubert" was whispered in the audience. He had hardly entered, but it seemed that one recognized him by his step, by his way of opening the door. And when, after this nostalgic cantilena in the minor, there followed the contrasted G major theme of the violoncellos, a charming song of almost Ländler-like intimacy, every heart rejoiced, as if, after a long separation, the composer himself were among us in person.

Nevertheless, the fact remains that even if we are able to recognize the basic elements and the technical and musical building blocks in a piece and recall playing them before in a different context, their particular and novel combinations in the work at hand may still be quite problematic. Passages which are relatively easy in themselves may become quite difficult when played in combination or succession. Some of the 'familiar' elements may have occurred less frequently in the past and may be remembered less vividly than others; the composer of the piece may not be as well known, or his style not as readily identifiable, as others. Therefore sightreading has to be practised—even though these terms appear contradictory—and with the same care as any other area of instrumental technique.

How is it possible to practise something which is, by definition, an unprepared, spontaneous activity? Simply by doing it: that is, by reading and playing a great deal of new or unfamiliar music at first sight. This particular mode of practice, however, still requires certain guidelines if sightreading is to become easier, more efficient and accurate, and at the same time offer greater enjoyment.

The guidelines for sightreading practice can be divided into two categories: a set of rules concerning mental preparation immediately preceding the actual playing (anticipation); and a second set of rules which comes into effect during the playing (control).

The steps in the mental preparation stage are practically identical with those in starting to learn a new piece (which, after all, has to be 'sightread' for the first time). In sightreading, these steps are much more condensed in time: they may take a few minutes at first, but as experience grows and the sightreading facility develops, it will take less and less time until eventually the whole process can be completed 'at a glance'—or in no more than five to fifteen seconds—depending on the length and complexity of the piece. Proficiency in sightreading, needless to say, also reduces considerably the time required to learn a new work.

Learning to have an initial mental 'bird's-eye view' of the whole work is the key to all successful sightreading.

10 Rules before Playing

(1)   Notice the composer's name and the title of the work for clues of style, character, and sometimes tempo.
(2)   Notice the tempo indication (if this is not in the title) and metronome mark. If the tempo is not clearly indicated, look further in the piece for a phrase or theme of unmistakable character; or find the most rapid passage which will determine the tempo in which the whole piece can be accurately and musically played.
(3)   Notice the key signature: major or minor key.
(4)   Notice the time signature and decide how to count.
(5)   Notice the dynamic marks.
(6)   Notice the expressive indications.

After this initial and rather obvious glance at the beginning of the piece, leaf through briefly and look over the whole movement or work to get a general impression of its characteristics. Continue to notice the dynamic and expressive marks, but look especially for, and make a mental note of the likely trouble spots, difficulties and unusual features in order to anticipate the most practical immediate solutions. Specifically, take the following remaining steps:

(7)   Look for any changes in tempo or time-signature, ritenutos, accelerandos, fermatas and any other changes from the steady tempo; note rests and *any repeats*.
(8)   Note the problematic rhythmical passages and take a moment to hum them correctly in your mind.
(9)   Do the same with the likely intonation problems; make a mental note of the most serviceable fingerings, think in patterns and groups of notes, with particular attention to the high passages. (You will be well advised to stay in position and avoid frequent shifts in sightreading.)
(10)   Look for possible bowing problems, off-string, or spiccato passages and awkward string-crossings, noting where you need the biggest sound. (Remember that the composer's phrasing marks are *not* necessarily bowing marks.)

10 Rules while Playing

(1)   Keep playing. Do not stop even if you have to miss notes or play a few wrong ones.
(2)   Keep your count at an even pace, maintaining a steady tempo unless otherwise indicated by the composer. Be aware of the beat, but subdivide it mentally in the rhythmically complicated passages—rhythmical accuracy and clarity and a steady tempo are even more important in

sightreading than accuracy of pitch. Keep going rhythmically in whatever tempo you set.

(3)   Read groups of notes, note-clusters or whole passages at a glance, not just single notes; instead of isolated letters, read words, sentences or paragraphs, as in speed-reading. Look for the patterns.

(4)   Read and observe the bowing and articulation marks, obeying the dynamic and expressive indications—the neglected areas of reading.

(5)   Be on the alert for such common mistakes as overlooking a sharp or flat later in the same measure when it is no longer indicated, forgetting to continue crescendos or diminuendos which carry over but are not printed again in the next line, and overlooking or not accurately observing rests.

(6)   Know the exact location of every note you are playing within each beat and each measure, feeling but not emphasizing strong and weak beats. Be aware of the placement of notes and phrases within the larger units of measures.

(7)   Look out for the familiar turns of phrases, modulations or cadences of the composer and of his period, and for other known musical elements, such as scales, arpeggios, and dotted rhythms. This will automatically bring into play the customary fingering or bowing solutions you have established in previous experience and in the practice of scales, patterns and various bowings.

(8)   Look and read ahead, always trying to divide your attention between the actual playing and the projecting of the next passage. As in riding a bike or driving a car, you must watch the road ahead for musical traffic lights and street-signs while handling your own actual progress, fast or slow . . . or stationary.

(9)   In ensemble sightreading, be aware of the other players and listen to hear whether your part calls for leading or following. Continually check that others on your road are travelling at the same speed, making your own speed clear, occasionally underlining the rhythm in general by the judicious application of accents and stresses.

(10) Read and play the **Music**, not merely the notes. Music should be a mother-tongue, a living language, clear and understandable, which can be 'spoken' and convey a meaning to others even when played at that first sight.

8   SIGHTREADING PRACTICE II: HIGH POSITIONS AND RHYTHMIC PROBLEMS

High Positions

Playing in the higher positions seems to be a particular sightreading problem to many string players and needs special attention and practice. The problem is analysed in two parts: reading and identifying the notes; and playing them.

In reading, the height of the separate, short leger lines can be confusing. To help overcome this, superimpose in your mind an imaginary auxiliary staff an octave above the E string pitch and see it in your 'mind's eye':

Reading the '8ve' sign, another source of the problem, is, in effect, a form of transposing, such as cellists have to do in some Beethoven quartets. Towards improving reading above the stave, practise scales and other material an octave higher than written, reading the music under an imaginary 8ve sign. Then practise the same in various different keys. This can be done on material found in the Kreutzer Studies, Tartini's *Art of Bowing*, or Sevcik's op. 8.

The Sevcik studies also make excellent ear-training material: they should be sung before playing (at first aloud, later mentally) to make sure that you hear the pitch in your head before actual playing. This is essential for string playing in general, and for sightreading in particular.

The actual playing can be improved in the higher positions not only by practising these scales and other exercises an octave higher, but by continually reading selected works written largely in the high positions, such as are found in Paganini's *Caprices* and Gavinies' *Matinées*. The goal in this kind of practice is to improve reading and, at the same time, tone quality and intonation. Even in sightreading, pay attention to the changing distance of the bow from the bridge (reduced proportionately with the reduced string-length), the proper combination of bow-speed and pressure at the proximity of the bridge, and to the reduced dimensions of the same intervals in higher positions. Knowing that you have to use these aspects of technique as soon as you see high positions coming, helps the eye and ear to prepare for them.

Rhythm

Incisive rhythm is an indispensable ingredient in any musical performance and particularly so in sightreading, where it is the foundation and safeguard for the continuity and intelligibility of unfamiliar musical texts.

(1) First and foremost, you must learn to maintain a steady tempo regardless of technical difficulty, rhythmical complexity or emotional excitement. Proper use of a metronome in sightreading is your first aid but you should not be merely the passive recipient of its beat; to profit from it, you must observe any tendency to slow down or speed up and then switch off the metronome to examine why. Is it a technical difficulty? If so, analyse the difficulty systematically. Is it from emotional excitement? If so, this may be acceptable as long as it is not exaggerated and is not directly against the composer's wishes or style. Is it rhythmical complexity?

Complexity of rhythm causes difficulty if you have not practised dividing the length of a beat in steady tempo and here a metronome is invaluable. Practice reading and counting the following with metronome, tapping or clapping without the instrument:

Now read and count again without the metronome, playing:

    (a)   détaché bows on a repeated note
    (b)   various bowings on scales
    (c)   détaché bows on scales
    (d)   slurred, legato bows on scales

Put the metronome on again after you have played (c) and (d) and play them again, looking at the examples but counting inwardly only. Once you are counting inwardly like this, you need only to be able to remember a metronome mark's beat to be able to dispense with a metronome altogether. This you can practise with your second aid: a non-digital wrist-watch. Most 'second' hands beat five times to each second so, looking at or listening to the watch, practise counting 'five' until you can memorize the rate of the single beats in a second. To check that you have finally memorized the rate properly, practise counting five-beat seconds as a unit without looking at the watch but checking after 10, 30 or 60 seconds, correcting your count when necessary. Once you have the beat firmly in your memory, you have your own metronome inside you and you can 'set' your personal metronome to the key marks normally used by composers like this:

$$4 \text{ beats of the watch} = \text{MM } 75$$
$$3 \text{ beats of the watch} = \text{MM } 100$$
$$2 \text{ beats of the watch} = \text{MM } 150$$

Counting in fives, MM = 60, and sub-dividing the unit into two beats of MM = 120 . . . you may soon surprise yourself in your ability to have a built-in 'steady tempo'.

(2) Next you need a guide to practise sightreading *changes* from the steady tempo, getting slower or faster.

(a) In ritenuto (ritardando, allargando) every beat should get gradually slower, each fraction of the beat proportionately longer. At a certain point of the ritenuto, especially a longer one, the beats may become too slow and far apart for correct judgement and control; this can be continued and assured by doubling the beat, switching to twice as fast a count at a strategic point:

Beat: ×   ×   × × × ×   × × × ×

(b) In accelerando (stringendo) the technique is used in the opposite direction, switching the beat to twice as slow at a critical point, when the pulse becomes too fast for practical counting:

Beat: ×   ×   ×   ×   ×   ×   ×   ×   ×

(Conductors use the same technique with the baton.)

Similar guidelines apply to less pronounced gradations of tempo changes (such as calando, calmando, cédez) or animando (pressez, augmentez). Work contrariwise: to get slower, double the beat to twice as fast; to get faster, halve the beat to twice as slow. This will assure much better control over such changes in the tempo: they can be more gradual, more logical musically and their rate of change foreseeable. That in turn will greatly help in ensemble playing.

(c) Rubato is a temporary suspension of the steady beat within the relatively even progress of the overall tempo. It is still a controlled flexibility of the beat in either direction, whether slowing down or moving ahead. Freedom of beat or tempo, if it is not to degenerate into chaos, also needs a certain control; without it rubato is nothing more than "musical sea-sickness" (Hanslick). True rubato arises from a need for extraordinary expressivity in a phrase or passage; it can be applied when a modulation or harmonic progress needs to be emphasized, or when the style of the composition requires it (eg parlando, recitativo). In all instances it must sound natural, spontaneous and inevitable, and has to follow its own speech-like inner logic. Rubato can be likened to a family taking a stroll during which the child keeps slowing down or stopping to look at this or that, and every so often skipping and running ahead to examine something else. Every time, however, he either catches up with his parents or slows down to wait for them, and the steady pace of the parents' walk remains unchanged. Rubato is of an improvisatory character which is impossible to notate and needs all the more discipline, particularly in sightreading, where it can be disguising uncertainty.

(d) Fermatas, when they occur during the piece, are temporary suspensions of the beat and momentarily stop the progress of the tempo. They might be called extreme examples of the agogic accent and are usually preceded or introduced by ritenutos. There are also some lesser interruptions in the tempo or beat, such as caesuras or luftpausas (') which are momentary hitches.

(3) Apart from a steady tempo and an awareness of controlled departures from it, there are important rhythmic signs to look for within that tempo:

(a) Rests, the stepchildren of the rhythm family, are often neglected, shortchanged or held inaccurately. The lack of physical activity during a rest should, on the contrary, be compensated for by heightened mental alertness if the rhythmical structure of the piece is to be maintained. Shabby treatment of rests is a frequent cause of rhythmical errors (and ensemble disasters): in slower tempi it is tempting to suspend the mental counting of the beats, to abandon the pulse or to stop following the other parts in the continuing music, thereby losing your place and the continuity of the piece. In faster tempi, short rests tend to be too long and the notes following them too late. To counter this play passages such as the following, actually omitting the rests and playing the notes on the beat:

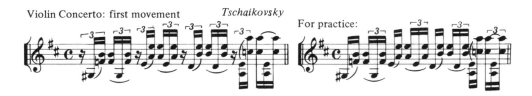

When you see a rest coming on a strong beat, a mental accent placed on it will help maintain the rhythmical structure:

(b)   Accents, which anchor down the rhythmical structure of a piece, reinforce it and make it clear; they also underline the changes and variations within that structure. In ensemble sightreading their correct application is particularly important. They need not be marked specifically in the music but a good sightreader will feel them coming in the music itself. Learn to differentiate two kinds of accent when you first read through a piece:

(i)   The dynamic accent, stressing a note by making it louder than its neighbours, on the beat.
(ii)   The agogic accent, stressing a note in time, either by delaying it after its neighbour or by holding on to it before releasing it to its neighbour.

The alternation of strong and weak accents is a fundamental characteristic of rhythm in general, and of musical rhythm in particular. One of Webster's definitions of rhythm is: 'the pattern of recurrent strong and weak accents, vocalization and silence and the distribution and combination of these elements in speech'. This definition is perfectly applicable to music and the hierarchy of these strong and weak accents (or beats) inherent in the various metres and measures is important to know and to observe. Learn to recognize beats in order of strength:

$\frac{2}{4}$ time: beat 1 2

$\frac{3}{4}$ time: beats 1 3 2

$\frac{4}{4}$ time: beats 1 3 4 2

Compound time follows the same order of strength:

$\frac{6}{8}$ time: beats 1 4

$\frac{9}{8}$ time: beats 1 7 4

$\frac{12}{8}$ time: beats 1 7 10 4

Syncopation is another form of accentuation, where the accent does not fall on the beat or on the normal strong point of the measure. Here, the accent is on the beginning of the note, regardless of which fraction of the beat it starts on. For an accurate and rhythmical execution of syncopated notes, even in a very fast tempo, it is useful to practise by mentally subdividing the beat into fractions indicated by the syncopation:

This is not to be confused with 'after-beats', which are off-beat notes alternating with on-the-beat rests of equal value which look like this:

Hemiola is another form of syncopation to look for, where two simultaneous rhythms form a ratio of 3 to 2:

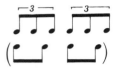

Practising Rhythm

The bow, by its nature, is the rhythmically more incisive element of string technique. The spontaneous articulation of the bow-change itself creates a certain rhythm which can be useful in underlining the rhythmical structure, but is not always easy to suppress: a smooth, unaccented bow-change is one of the great challenges of string technique. The left-hand fingers in contrast need constant training and exercise to develop and maintain their clear and strong articulating ability. This articulation, in turn, is more difficult when lifting the fingers than in placing them on the fingerboard. Evenness of articulation is further complicated by the fact that our fingers are of uneven length.

(1) A good way to correct a tendency to uneven articulation is to compensate for the error in the opposite direction. If, in a passage of even note-values, you tend to play some notes longer than others, play these shorter than their normal values, and then even them out:

This applies not only to the left hand in legato passages, but also to the bow when it is uneven in détaché, spiccato, or string crossings. Depending on the direction of the unevenness, these passages can be equalized like this:

To play: practice:

A E A D   or

To play: practice:

E A D A   or

If uneven articulation is a particular weakness, it is useful to practise actually playing the opposites so that the physical movements of the bow or fingers will help your eye to sightread even note-values correctly.

(2)   Watch out for dotted rhythms, which are often not sharp enough, especially in legato. Rhythm (a) here often becomes (b) and should be practised (c) to counteract the mistake:

(a)   (b)   (c)

Sloppy dotted rhythms in legato are commonly produced when a string change is involved ... so beware of them. Make sure also that legato dotted rhythms really are *legato*. Rhythms (a) and (b) here often sound as in (c) and (d):

(a)   (b)   (c)   (d)

and need particular care.

(3)   Look for the pitfall of tied notes. The note following a tie is often too late and too short. Rhythm (a) here may carelessly sound (b) or (c) and the 'opposite' to imagine (or physically play for practice) is (d):

Sonata No.3   *Brahms*
(a)   (b)   (c)   (d)

Rhythm and rhythmical problems have to be practised just as carefully and intensely as any other phase of instrumental technique, and rhythmical sense has to be kept in practice just as much as good intonation or any other technical facility. If you take the trouble to practise sightreading systematically on the lines suggested in the last two chapters, you will learn to get a good idea of a new work at a glance, technically and musically. You will avoid false starts, reduce the practice time and, above all, take much of the drudgery out of purely mechanical periods of practice.

9   MEMORY PRACTICE I: FIRST STEPS

Difficulties in memorizing and fears of slips in memory are widespread amongst aspiring performers. Too often, the solution is thought to be in endless practice until the sheer number of repetitions provide a performance 'by heart'—temporary, seldom reliable, and certainly not from the heart. 'Forgetting' is in most cases not a defect of memory but of perception. It is not that you forget what comes next; it is that you did not know well enough, in practice, what comes next. Your memory does not know *what to remember*, or, in computer terms, it has not been properly programmed.

The brain can register events, facts and impressions. It can retain and store them. It can recognize and recall them at a later date. So there are three first steps to practise in memorizing:

(1)   Learn to maximize what you see and hear when you first read a new piece, following the basic rules of sightreading (see page 63).
(2)   Learn to put every phase of this initial registration into your practice, stored in the memory at each stage.
(3)   Distinguish between recognition and recall:

   (a)   *recognition* is when you can read a piece fluently *with* music.
   (b)   *recall* is when you can play the piece fluently *without* music.

Inadequate initial observation, insufficient technical information, and superficial understanding all add up to faulty recall. You may easily remember parts of a piece if they have left a particular imprint on your brain, but you must practise those parts which have *not* left this imprint vividly in your first preparation.

Scientists tell us that the storage capacity of the brain is virtually limitless and that it probably retains everything it experiences; that memory capacity actually expands the more things are remembered; and that we don't even begin to make full use of our brain's capabilities. The brain is a wonderfully complex organism which functions by electric impulses and chemical reactions or changes. It is far better than any computer, not only because its storage capacity for information and general efficiency is much greater than any computer yet devised, but also because it comprehends such concepts as ethics, aesthetics and style . . . and registers emotions. It is capable—as no computer is—of *imagination*, which allows it to undertake many other intellectual, emotional and physical activities such as composing and interpreting music, while it can also oversee and direct the technical and physical elements of its performance.

Since the brain retains everything it experiences, memory problems simply mean that we are not using our given capabilities fully or correctly. If you don't remember something you have heard or read, saw or did, or something which 'happened' to you, it means that it has not left a sufficiently deep or vivid imprint on your mind, that you have not absorbed or registered it on a high enough level of intensity to recall it. Your brain was not alert or 'alive' enough, to leave the mind open to all the relevant impressions and observations which made up the event. We remember best that which interests us most.

Failure at this first stage of the memory process is often compounded by poor practice habits at the later stages. There are five aspects of memory to think about:

(1) Sensory, through the eye (usually strongest), the ear and the fingers.
(2) Factual, through the assimilation of something you have not met or heard before.
(3) Episodic, through a conscious recognition of something you have met or heard before.
(4) Skilled, through the kinetic ability to repeat something you have done before.
(5) Semantic, through analysis of style, structure and expression.

10 First Steps

(1) Read the music without the instrument. Even if you have never heard the piece before, get an idea of how it should ideally sound by reading the music and hearing it in your head (silent sight-singing). This way your eventual performance will tend to rise to this very high standard set mentally, rather than stay close to the necessarily lower level of a premature and imperfect immediate play-through with the instrument. Make a mental note of all the places which might be problematic technically or musically, and reason why. Be aware of the musical and interpretative concept from the beginning.
(2) Decide, still without the instrument, and set down on paper all the fingerings and bowings you can, without actually playing. With experience, you will eventually be able to choose most of them in this way, without having to change too many later on. Make a blueprint of, and visualize the work's architecture, form and musical divisions.

(3)   Register and spell these out in your mind ('mentalize') as you begin slow practice *with* the instrument. Include all pertinent information, technical and musical interrelation you can think of, to strengthen your basic knowledge of the piece.

(4)   Give yourself an idea, as soon as you begin to play the piece reasonably accurately, of what it will mean actually to perform it, by playing it through in concert tempo, even if imperfectly and with music. Add this knowledge to your store of information to be memorized.

(5)   Single out the particularly difficult parts for more intensive study, but do not neglect the easy ones: they are also important for the memory.

(6)   Organize the material to be memorized into musically coherent but shorter units—the brain remembers best a limited amount of new information at a time. Add a new unit each time one has been memorized until they add up to the complete piece.

(7)   Use other associations. One association will evoke many others. Make up a scenario or a story, for example, in which the turn of events or images correspond more or less closely to the melodic, harmonic or expressive direction of the piece. As if writing an opera in reverse you are given the music and have to write the libretto. As the story unfolds, it will remind you of the music.

(8)   Use Mnemonics. This is the term for a variety of techniques and devices which help memory. In a sense any method which helps you to memorize better is a form of mnemonic. Certainly the use of strong associations, as in (7) above, is one form of mnemonic. But there are also more artificial or mechanical mnemonics to be used:

> (a)   Fingerings. In similar, but differently continuing passages, deliberately use different fingerings to lead into the different continuations. (This is particularly helpful in memorizing 18th-century music.)
>
> (b)   Repetitions. Count the number of times a passage is repeated and repeat the count mentally as you practise.
>
> (c)   Anchors. Remember a particularly vivid or unusual note as an anchor to hold the rest of the passage together.
>
> (d)   Markers. Take a certain note *or* finger *or* bowing and place it accurately in your memory as being on a certain beat in a measure.
>
> (e)   Cues. Note a passage on another instrument in concert or ensemble playing and note the number of beats or bars until your next entry.

(9)   Practise performing the piece. Memorize the physical motions you use. There are additional lessons to be learned and memorized: different motions, energy output, stamina, muscular feelings, and your own emotional state of mind. Play it often, and if possible with a good

accompanist: the piano part is also an integral part of the piece you are memorizing.

(10)   Perform it as if in concert, with instrument, by memory and with full projection of all expression and temperament...in concert attire!

Keep these memorizing sessions relatively short, depending on your powers of concentration, interrupted by rest periods of about ten minutes. It is a characteristic of the brain that it retains things best and is most receptive at the beginning and at the end of such working sessions. By taking frequent rests between memorizing sessions, these most productive periods of the mind are multiplied. Review frequently the parts just learned, and on the next day start again with a review of all the work previously done.

In approaching the problems of memorizing, however, it needs to be underscored that outstanding and inspired performances do occur while playing with music, and that great performances are not the solely patented outcome of the music having been memorized. In fact, the initial steps in learning a new work *parallel the initial steps in memorizing*, whether a piece is ultimately played by memory or not. Nor is a 'good memory' a necessary pre-requisite of musicianship. Most chamber-music performers (and, of course, orchestral musicians) use music, and, in fact, the rule should be that either all or none of the ensemble participants should play by memory. (Sonata teams, especially, please note: otherwise there is an undesirable element of 'display for show' on the part of the lone dissenter.)

Using music in performance, stopping short of complete recall, is not evidence of poor initial observation and registration, incomplete preparation or knowledge, or poor practice habits. It can be the outward sign of a different musical goal with no diminishing of excellence. Proper preparation and practice, leading to an outstanding performance with the use of music, means that even if 'memorizing' has not been achieved consciously, the performer is very close to it, or could complete it with little effort—he is not utterly dependent on having to read the music.

10 MEMORY PRACTICE II: ANTICIPATION

Anticipation is the ability of the mind (in 'imagination') to foresee actions, motions, events, feelings and impressions based on previous experience, and project them into the future. To anticipate, according to the dictionary, is 'to foresee and act in advance'. It is the obverse of memory, projecting the present into the immediate future, while you are actually playing the instrument.

Our day-to-day physical and mental activities depend on this ability to foresee, prepare and set in motion the next task, even while performing the current one. In walking, eating or speaking, each action carries within it the seeds of the next, and a trigger mechanism in the subconscious mind sets in motion the next phase during the current phase, in a kind of *mental chain reaction.*

This simultaneous mental and physical activity of two or more sequential actions or motions makes possible the continuous, fluid and uninterrupted functions of our everyday life. Try walking in a very slow motion: while one leg is still in the air, the other already flexes the appropriate muscles and is getting ready to push off as the first returns to the ground—all in one uninterrupted, fluid movement. When you eat, you open your mouth as the hand with the fork approaches it, *before* it actually reaches it.

In most everyday activities this process has become automatic from early childhood, to the point where we no longer pay attention to, or are even, conscious of it. Yet, though the success of such less natural and more complicated activities as playing an instrument (or playing any ball game really well) depends even more on the perfect functioning of this anticipatory ability, very little attention has been paid to its mental development in practice studies. Anticipation is important in the technical approach to playing an instrument, but *crucial* in memorizing.

The ability to anticipate is present to a different degree in different persons. Some youngsters can pick up a bat or a tennis racquet (or a violin bow) for the first time and handle it with a naturalness of motion, grace and fluidity which can only be accounted for by an innate ability to anticipate mentally which results in perfect physical coordination. But for those without this natural ability (or for those players whose technical problems limit its function), many difficulties will never disappear unless this 'anticipation' can be developed by practice. Theoretically, a shift from first to eighth position should be as easy as eating or tying a shoelace in the dark ... given anticipation and practice.

Anticipation for a string player can mean:

(1)   Hearing the pitch of every note ahead, singly and in groups.
(2)   Feeling in advance the particular finger on the right string in the right position.
(3)   Feeling any change of bow ahead.
(4)   Judging the pressure, speed and amount of bow needed ahead.
(5)   Judging the time needed to get to a new position in any tempo.
(6)   Judging the distance between two positions of a coming shift.
(7)   Eventually, hearing whole passages to come and the sequence of fingers and bow needed.

Fortunately, while all these characteristics are distinct and identifiable elements of each note, they are still merely the different facets of the same entity, and cannot be thought of separately except in the very beginning of our learning process. In this respect anticipation parallel, closely the 'mentalizing' stage.

How to 'Mentalize' a New Piece

Looking at these few bars, what can you see and remember before you even play them?

Key: E minor.
Time and Mood: ₵; Allegro molto appassionato; MM c. = 96–100.
Wait: One-and-a-half measures, introduction.
Begin: *piano*, middle of measure, dotted rhythm on *b″* up-beat, up-bow. (Use no more than half bow to avoid unwanted accent, feel light weight, 'floating' bow arm.) Left hand: third finger, second position on E string (feel the place on the string). Notice the eighth-note (quaver) figure in the accompaniment, which will have to fit with your melody.
Bar 3:   Major third down to first finger: about $\frac{2}{3}$ down bow. Shift first finger through silent *b″* up major 3rd to extended third finger *e‴*: $\frac{1}{3}$ bow, leaving $\frac{2}{3}$ for
Bar 4:   First two notes, first finger. Stretch fourth finger to *g‴*.
Bar 5:   Pull fourth finger back to *f♯‴*, *e″* with third finger, first finger to *c‴* (still in same hand position), repeat *e‴* and

81

Bar 6:   Reach back slightly to *b'''* with first finger again. Note that *f#'''* in bar 5 was the top of the melodic arc—tip of the bow—and having started back, up-bow, using almost the whole bow, you must adjust its speed in the *b'''* for the next phrase. . . .

These are just a few of the features you can study in the first six bars even before you practise: when you are playing, they will then be in your sub-conscious and function automatically. They will, however, be *secure* because of the early detail in memorizing and no emergency—such as a difference from a set tempo, an out-of-tune string or a slippery fingerboard—will disturb that security.

Just as there are different types of memories, there are different types of memorizing abilities. Some individuals have near total or even 'photographic' memories, super-capacities to observe and absorb automatically and instinctively—they don't need to enumerate all this information consciously or to mentalize it, it happens spontaneously. Others, the great majority, have to work at improving their ability to do this. But with good mental and physical practice habits, memory and memorizing in all three stages can be trained to a very high degree.

How to Anticipate

Follow the sketch opposite:

When, after, very slow and very strict practice, this process has become fluent and spontaneous, and when the control phase has become reliable and instantaneous, gradually increase the tempo until the anticipating, playing, judging and correcting the note has become almost simultaneous and automatic, as in:

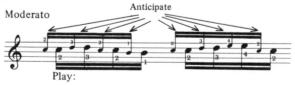

Then progress to the automatic anticipation of larger units, groups of notes and passages, depending on the tempo and velocity of the passages. Anticipation in such larger groups of notes includes not only the sequence of left-hand fingers, but finger-patterns, multiple shifts, and bow-patterns, as in:

Here, anticipation of the next group springs to the mind towards the end of the group being played.

Remember that, while the actual speed of playing increases, frequency of 'command' remains relatively constant, but contains proportionately more information in each command (or anticipatory) unit.

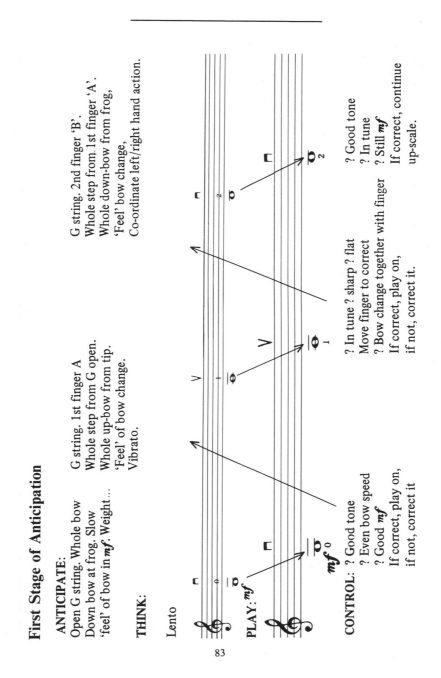

First Stage of Anticipation

ANTICIPATE:
Open G string. Whole bow
Down bow at frog. Slow
'feel' of bow in *mf*. Weight...

G string. 1st finger A
Whole step from G open.
Whole up-bow from tip.
'Feel' of bow change.
Vibrato.

G string. 2nd finger 'B'.
Whole step from 1st finger 'A'.
Whole down-bow from frog,
'Feel' bow change,
Co-ordinate left/right hand action.

THINK:

Lento

PLAY: *mf*

CONTROL: ? Good tone
? Even bow speed
? Good *mf*
If correct, play on,
if not, correct it

? In tune ? sharp ? flat
Move finger to correct
? Bow change together with finger
If correct, play on,
if not, correct it.

? Good tone
? In tune
? Still *mf*
If correct, continue
up-scale.

Final Stages of Study, Learning and Memorizing

3 Stages of Memory:

I   Initial perception; observation and registration. Information gathering; mentalizing. Indispensable basis of Good Memory.

II   Retention, storage and reinforcement:

III   Performance:
(a) Recognition (with music)
(b) Recall (by memory)

10 Steps toward better memorizing:

(1) Read music without instrument, observe, be aware of musical content from start.

(2) Decide bowings and fingerings, still without instrument.

(3) Start slow practice with instrument; register in your mind all impressions, information, connections—MENTALIZE.

(4) Try playing in tempo in early stages with instrument.

(5) Practise intensely the difficult parts, but don't neglect the easy ones.

(6) Divide the work into shorter segments for better retention.

(7) Re-connect shorter segments, fit into context of form and interpretation; put unneeded facts into the back of the mind.

(8) Practise performing, with accompaniment, still with music, if needed.

(9) Play entire work through in your mind, without instrument or music, recall everything vividly which pertains to actual performance.

(10) Play by memory a complete 'concert' performance.

Cue-words to remember:

Read
Realize
Remark
Register
Record
Relate
Retain

Reinforce
Repeat
Retrace
Reconstruct
Reassemble
Reconnect
Rehearse
Recognize

Remember
Recall
Reproduce
Recreate

Notes on the Final Stages of Study, Learning and Memorizing

(1)   Make sure you have practised Stage I of Memory thoroughly before you go on to II, and Stage II thoroughly before you go on to III.

(2)   Of the 10 Steps, (1) and (2) are mental preparation; (3) to (8) are practical; (9) and (10) are mental *and* practical.

(3)   Ask yourself if you have really considered all the cue-words in your practice, before you are satisfied that you have a piece 'by heart'.

11 PRACTISING THE OBVIOUS

Certain seemingly trivial matters, when neglected, can lead to disproportionately serious difficulties. So add to your practising:

The Platform Posture

A piece should be practised in the posture in which it is to be performed. If you are to be seated, as in most ensemble and orchestral playing, pay careful attention to a comfortable and healthy posture:

> (1)   Choose a chair, if possible, with its seat parallel to the floor, and at a height which allows your knees to be level with the seat, or slightly slanting forward.
> (2)   Keep the upper body in the same posture as when playing standing; the only difference is that the legs are bent and the weight of the body is on the seat instead of on the heels.
> (3)   Do not lean back in the chair, sit forward; the muscles of your back must be free to participate in your movements together with the other muscles of the upper body.
> (4)   Slouching, even if a temporary relief, is a sure cause of future back problems by bending the column of vertebrae too far out of alignment. The back of the chair should not be too deep for those few moments when you don't play and can lean against it temporarily.

Whether you are to play standing or seated, always hold the violin level with the shoulder so that the bow does not have to operate on a slope (with a tendency to slide away from the bridge). In solo playing see that the instrument is parallel with the edge of the platform so that everyone in the audience can see and hear you equally well.

The Music Stand

This can be another source of problems. When playing standing, the music stand should be high enough so that the middle of the page can be at eye level. It is astonishing that in this age of ever taller generations it is nearly impossible to find music stands which are high enough for anyone above the average height! The music stand should also be directly in front of the player, with the violin held to the left at an angle of approximately 45 degrees. The player should 'face' the music and avoid the 'peek-a-boo' stance, turning or twisting the body neither left nor right. Playing in a seated position, set the stand only high enough to see the music comfortably and still have the conductor, or your colleagues opposite, in the line of vision. Sharing an orchestral stand, agree the height and direction with your partner before rehearsal starts and check it after the break.

The Instrument

(1)   For a secure but un-squeezed bow-hold it is very important that the space between the upper end of the frog and the leather grip covering the silver or whale-bone wrapping of the stick should fit the thumb; the distance should be neither too small (or non-existent) nor too great, normally about $\frac{1}{4}$ inch. In the absence of this support, the thumb will slip either too far or ever higher on the stick, making the player feel about to drop the bow. In trying to prevent losing it, you will squeeze too hard with the thumb and the other fingers, causing cramps and even more insecurity in holding and handling the bow. As the hair gets longer with use and, particularly in humidity, it is prudent to ask for short hair when having the bow rehaired.

(2)   Watch that the leather grip itself has not worn off; its slight ridge, together with the edge of the frog, provides the essential support to the thumb and allows a secure bow-hold without tension or stiffness. Simple attention to this elementary problem can often cure what seem to be insurmountable and frustrating difficulties in bow technique.

(3)   Use rosin on the bow hair evenly all along between frog and tip, and not only at the frog and near the tip, where it is least used. The rosin should be used often and a little at a time; otherwise most of it will end up on the strings (which is not the idea), coating and choking them and preventing them from vibrating freely. The resulting poor tone quality may again be attributed to problems of complicated origin when, in fact, it can dramatically improve by simply following this elementary and common-sense rule of instrumental hygiene: *clean* the strings after *every* playing.

Your Frame of Mind

Although the brain tries to fulfil any image or goal set for it, it tends to receive what it expects to receive and to reject what it is not expecting. This is known as mental 'set': a deliberate setting for a positive goal—positive thinking—should always be your aim. Be clear about your objectives and visualize them actually happening.

Mental practice can accomplish amazing things: from improved performance in sports (Olympic champions are known to have practised their speciality this way) to the astonishing feats of physical and physiological control of mind over matter and body by fakirs or yogis. Experiments have shown that a group of basket-ball players practising purely mentally have increased their accuracy at the same rate as another group practising the actual target-shooting. Further, it has been found that when one practises physical motions mentally, or imagines an activity to be taking place, small electrical changes can be detected in the associated muscles even if there is no physical sign of movement.

But mental training not only affects the muscles and improves performance. It also increases confidence by preparing you thoroughly for a given situation, improving your self-image, and encouraging you to aim high. A performer with well-founded self-confidence radiates and projects this confident image, and instantly influences the audience. Do not forget that the audience begins to judge you as a performer, whether consciously or not, from the moment you enter the stage and before you ever play a note. A positive reaction can in turn come back from the audience in undefinable but very real waves encouraging and inspiring you to the highly accomplished performance for which your positive practice has trained you.

A SYSTEMATIC TABLE
OF FINGER PATTERNS

Here is the complete list, in the basic settings, of all four fingers on one string:

Category I

In this category, the range of the four fingers does not exceed an augmented fourth (normal and contracted positions) and the progression between fingers is stepwise.

Pattern 1

as found in
Partita No.3 in E: Preludio

J. S. Bach

Pattern 2

as found in
Partita No. 1 in B minor: last movement

J. S. Bach

Pattern 3

as found in
Sonata No. 2 in C: Andante

J. S. Bach

 and

Pattern 4

as found in
Caprice No. 24   *Paganini*   Violin Concerto No. 2: first movement   *Wieniawski*

(Pattern without 4th finger)

Pattern 5

as found in
Violin Concerto No. 2: third movement

Bartok

sul D

Pattern 6

as found in
Violin Concerto: first movement

Brahms

90

Pattern 7

as found in

(Pattern without 4th finger)

Category II

In this category the range between first and fourth finger is from a perfect fifth to a minor sixth and some of the intervals between neighbouring fingers are more than an augmented second.

Pattern 8

as found in
Violin Concerto No.4, K.218:
first movement

Pattern 9

as found in
Chaconne

91

Pattern 10

as found in
Violin Concerto
first movement

Mendelssohn
third movement

Pattern 11

as found in
Sonata in D, op.94a: *Prokofiev*
first movement

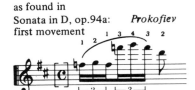

Caprice No.15   *Paganini*

Pattern 12

as found in
Caprice No. 17

Paganini

Pattern 13

as found in
Violin Concerto: first movement   *Brahms*

Pattern 14

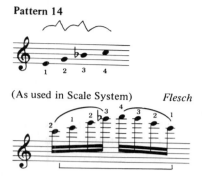

(As used in Scale System)   *Flesch*

Category III

In this category are rarely used greater extensions and more unusual spacing of fingers. These more advanced combinations—as with some in the second category above—occur more often in virtuoso works. They are more prevalent and easier to play in the higher positions where the range of the hand is increased.

Pattern 15

Pattern 16

Pattern 17

Pattern 18

Pattern 19

Pattern 20

Pattern 21

Finally, there is the notorious chord known as the 'Paganini stretch' probably the most extreme extension feasible on the violin:

Transferred to one string, it would give the following pattern:

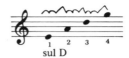

sul D

An undercurrent of this pattern concept, whether conscious or intuitive, can be discerned in the compositions of many violinists-composers such as Paganini and Ysaÿe, whose musical thinking was influenced by idiomatic instrumental writing. Other extreme and unusual examples can sometimes be found in the literature and a few more combinations can be arrived at by sheer mathematical permutations. Their use, however, would be either impossible or impractical.

The Advantages of the Complete System

(1)   The **Gridiron** with its 100 spaces constitutes a yardstick to measure distances of the fingerboard more precisely, and the visual representation of this framework will give a tangible reference to recognize and identify any note instantly. This instant identification of where to place each note will reduce by an all-important split second the time needed to recognize, and play accordingly, the printed symbol.

(2)   The **Pattern System**, superimposed on this gridiron, will enable the brain to direct the fingers more securely and accurately to their proper slot on the fingerboard, now no longer an empty, unmarked surface; and, by simplifying and reducing all passages to their essentials, it will cut down the amount of time needed for practice to learn any work. The use of patterns helps string technique physically and psychologically: playing clusters instead of single notes, thinking of groups of notes as larger units, and connecting these groups as units, reduces the number of separate mental commands and physical motions, increases speed and accuracy, reduces muscular tension and creates a less hectic frame of mind.

(3)   **Intonation** will become more accurate through the use of patterns, not only by more accurate fingering but by better hearing: in correlating the pitches of a greater number of notes, you will hear and judge each pitch, not only singly, but in relation to the other notes and pitches in the group and to its place in the overall harmony.

(4)   **Memory** will be more secure by providing the left hand with a structural framework that is underpinned both mentally and visually.

(5)   **Interpretation** will be more perceptive from a bird's-eye view of the

basic material and components, the inner shape, and the interrelations of the musical structure.

(6)   **Sightreading** will dramatically improve as you begin to think in larger units, recognize a passage as 'pattern X fingered in position Y' and play it immediately. This is the essence of sightreading, the musical equivalent of speed-reading.

(7)   **Ensemble playing** will be easier as you will be able to concentrate on the ensemble as a whole, released from thinking too much about left hand technical problems.

(8)   **Stage fright** will be reduced as your left hand technique has a precise, detailed and visual foundation on which to rely, removing the insecurity and unpredictability that can suddenly produce panic in a performance.

A COMPREHENSIVE TABLE
OF SHIFTS

It is possible to cover the whole length of the violin fingerboard and to go from the lowest note to the highest without any shift at all, merely by using extensions and contractions:

Strings: G - - - D - - - A - - - E - - -

... but it is not very practical. The range of virtually every work in the violin literature requires that the left hand moves from one spot on the fingerboard to another in such a way that the hand and arm muscles remain comfortable and capable of playing all the notes cleanly and in tune. In other words, we have to 'shift' and 'change positions'.

The various changes of positions serve one of two different purposes (with an occasional combination of the two) either by choice or by necessity:

(1)   shifts for purely technical reasons and purposes, and
(2)   shifts for expressive purposes.

Technical shifts are dictated by the need to go from one position to another, usually in rapid and clearly articulated passages emphasizing the more instrumental characteristics of the violin. These shifts should be articulated as cleanly as possible: the slide connecting the positions should be inaudible, the motion itself made relatively quickly and adjusted to the speed of the passage itself.

Expressive shifts, on the other hand, try to approximate to the quality of the singing human voice and bring out the lyric and emotional quality of both the instrument and the music itself. In this type of shift, used usually in slower tempi or between notes of longer value, the slide connecting the two notes is more or less audible (depending on style and tempo), much as the human voice bridges the gap between two different pitches in expressive legato singing. The choice between one type of shift and the other also reflects individual preference in a given style, but there is no reason why a purely technical shift should not be played in an expressive way.

Mechanically speaking, the simplest way to go from one position to another is by sliding with the same finger:

All the other kinds of shifts, involving two different fingers, are merely variations of this. They can be classified into three groups:

(1) 'Lead-shifts', which lead to the next position by sliding the finger playing the initial note of the shift until it reaches the note it *would* play in the new position; as you reach this new position, put the other finger, playing the note at the end of the shift, down on the string with *no* further sliding:

The silent note reached by the sliding finger can be called a 'bridge-note', or 'guide-note'. (Good practice for this may be found in Sevcik's Studies, op. 8.)

(2) 'End-shifts', in which the finger playing the note on which the shift *ends*, takes over immediately from the finger playing the initial note and does all the sliding until it reaches the end-note. The bridge note here is the one which the sliding finger *would* create if you let it sound at the point when it first touches the string at the beginning of the slide. These bridge or guide notes should be so short as to be almost inaudible in both kinds of shifts, more especially in end-shifts, where they should *never* sound.

It should also be noted that end-shifts are practically never used in downward directions (that is, from a higher position to a lower one) and that they are best done by neighbouring fingers.

97

(3)   Both kinds of shifts in combination, usually when there is a bow change during the shift something like this:

Shifts can be further differentiated between those done on the same bow and those during which the bow is changed. In the latter, the timing of the bow change and its co-ordination with the left-hand motion is very important and must be clear in the player's mind.

Shifts from higher to lower positions are more difficult than shifts upward because, in downward shifts, the motion of the arm pulls the instrument away from the player, needing a firmer grip on the instrument between chin and shoulder (or collarbone) and increasing muscular tension. The arm motion in upward shifts pushes the instrument toward the player, reinforcing the support. Holding the instrument level, or in a relatively horizontal position, can minimize these differences, but downward shifts need more practice than upward.

Always remember that the speed of a shift dictates the action required and bear this in mind when you practise slowly and then 'up to tempo'. You need three quite different actions to pass or hit a ball to someone else from a standing, jogging or running position: so you need to practise shifts accordingly.

A 'position' is defined by I. M. Yampolsky in his excellent book *The Principles of Violin Fingering* as:

> that position of the left hand, defined by the relation of the thumb and first finger, from which it is possible to play a given succession of notes without moving the hand and the *location* of the position is defined by the distance of the first finger from the nut.

The purpose of shifting, then, is to connect these various 'positions' by changing their 'location'.

These changes of positions, or shifts, occur in a variety of circumstances, for different reasons and often for different purposes. The following Table of Shifts undertakes to organize all these various types of shifts into a chart which makes the selection and execution of specific changes of positions easier. As the System of Finger-patterns organizes the left hand activities in their 'vertical' (or *across* the fingerboard) motions in the same position, so the Table of Shifts organizes the left hand actions in their 'horizontal' (or *along* the fingerboard) motions in different positions.

Technical Shifts: Single Notes

(1)   Upward Shifts, from lower to higher position.

(a) from lower finger to higher finger (1–2, 2–4, etc.):

are 'Lead-shifts' (see page 97). For practice, play out the 'bridge' note with the initial finger; in performance, the 'bridge' note is silent.

(b) from higher finger to lower finger (2–1, 3–1, etc.):

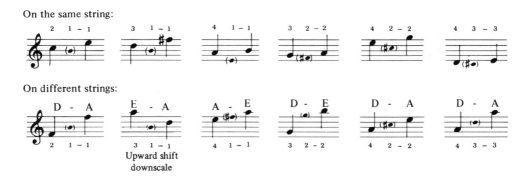

are 'End-shifts' (see page 97). Close the gap as much as possible between the two fingers if it is more than a half-step. This type of shift is used very often in scales and arpeggios. (Shifting with the higher finger in lower position would produce an audible, higher-pitched bridge-note unacceptable to the ear.) In shifts on different strings, the shifting finger slides on the string on which the end-note is played; the bridge note and slide are still silent. (Occasionally, you may find a lead-shift is also possible.)

99

(2) Downward Shifts, from higher to lower position:

    (a) from higher finger to lower finger (4–3, 2–1, etc.):

On the same string:

On different strings:

are lead-shifts. Shift with the initial finger until it reaches the lower position, then put down the end-note finger without any further sliding. In shifts covering two different strings, shift with the initial finger on initial string.

    (b) from lower finger (high position) to higher finger (low position):

On the same string:

On different strings:

are also lead-shifts, made in the same way as 2(a). The silent bridge-note is often a lower pitch than the end-note.

(Scale System)   *Flesch*

Technical Shifts: Double Stops

    (1) Upward Shifts, from lower to higher position, in thirds:

        (a) from lower pair of fingers to higher pair:

100

On the same strings: $\frac{1-2}{3-4}$ are made as 1 - 2 or 3 - 4 in single note shifts

(b) from higher pair of fingers to lower pair:

On the same strings: $\frac{2-1}{4-3}$ are made as 2 - 1 or 4 - 3 in single note shifts

On different pairs of strings: the shift is done with *one* finger, the finger which is on the *middle* string. It then follows the rules of single-note shifts. For example, from lower pair of fingers to higher pair:

and from higher pair of fingers to lower pair:

Upward shift
downscale

(2) Downward Shifts, from higher to lower positions, in thirds:

(a) from higher pair of fingers to lower pair:

On the same strings:
$\frac{2-1}{4-3}$ are made as 2 - 1 or 4 - 3 in single note shifts

(b) from lower pair of fingers to higher pair:

On the same strings:
$\frac{1-2}{3-4}$ are made as 1 - 2 or 3 - 4 in single note shifts

101

On different pairs of strings: the shift is done with the single finger on the middle string and follows the rules of single-note shifts. For example, from higher pair of fingers to lower pair:

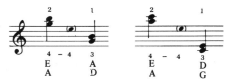

and from lower pair of fingers to higher pair:

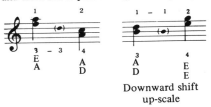

Downward shift
up-scale

(3) Shifts in other double stops:

(a) in Sixths

The same rules apply as for thirds:

(b) in Octaves with 1–4:

The same rules apply as for same-finger shifts:

Violin Concerto: first movement   *Beethoven*

(c) in Fingered Octaves

The same rules apply as for thirds:

(d) in Tenths

102

The same rules apply as for octaves with 1-4:

Caution: For extensions such as tenths and fingered octaves, the hand should be in a middle position from which both the forth *and* the first finger extends in opposite directions; otherwise the excessive strain on the overstretched fourth finger and wrist could cause cramp and damage tendons and muscles.

Technical Shifts Beginning or Ending on an Open String

In this type of shift the change of position is done in most cases while playing the open string, the shift being guided by the thumb and, sometimes, the base of the fore-finger as well. To practise the accuracy of the shift both lead-shifts and end-shifts can be used upwards, but only lead-shifts downwards.

(1)   Upward shifts on the same string:

   (a) Lead-shift:

   The guide finger (usually the first) is placed on a neighbouring string (preferably a higher one) at the pitch it would play in the position preceding the shift. It then moves, during the playing of the open string, until it reaches the position of the end-note.
   (b) End-shift:

   This type of shift is included here for practising purposes only. The open string, in effect, takes the place of the lower finger, usually the first.

(2)   Upward shifts on different strings:

(a) Lead-shift:

Slide with the lead-finger on the string where the end-note is located.

(b) End-shift:

Slide with the end-finger on the string where the end-note is located.

(3)   Downward shifts on the same string:

Shift with the finger of the upper note until it reaches, approximately, the first position (or the position of the note following the open string).

(4)   Downward shifts on different strings:

Move as for (3) above, but slide on the string of the top note.

Technical Shifts Between Notes of Identical Pitch

(1)   On the same string:

(2)   On different strings:

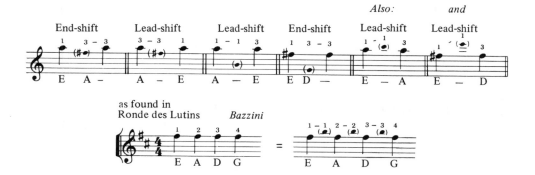

Expressive Shifts

Expressive shifts (see page 96), are a form of romantic expression and should mostly be used in music from the Romantic period onwards. In them, the slide is audible; they can be lead-shifts or end-shifts, but they need great care in determining the right choice.

(1) Lead-shifts:

    (a) Do not stop on, or otherwise emphasize the bridge-note (no human would sing that way), but glide over it:

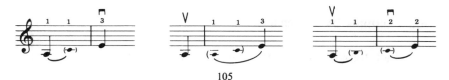

    (b) Slow down the bow slightly during the shift, reducing the pressure both from the bow and from the sliding finger.
    (c) Put the end-finger down as soon as the sliding finger arrives at the destination. The end-finger itself must not slide, but be placed squarely on pitch.
    (d) Be sure that the end-note gets full vibrato: it is the expressive object of the shift.
    (e) If a bow-change is involved, decide exactly the timing of the change. This may be an individual choice or preference, but should not be left up to chance. In lead-shifts it is better to change the bow after the shift, otherwise it is difficult to avoid repeating the initial note.

(f) The note *preceding* the shift should be emphasized whenever that note is on a heavy, or relatively heavy, beat. Usually, such notes are higher than that to which the shift leads, as in:

(2)   End-shifts:

The end-finger, which does the sliding, takes over from the initial finger at the beginning of the slide, but for a while the two fingers move together, very much like two runners before they pass the baton in a relay race. The sliding finger should land gradually on the string, attaining full finger-pressure only when reaching the end-note to avoid the bridge note sounding.

If there is a bow-change during this type of shift, it is best done at the beginning of the shift (a) and never at the end (b):

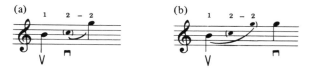

Occasionally you can change the bow in the middle of such a shift combining, in effect, lead-shift and end-shift:

Bow changes during such shifts should be as unnoticeable as possible: reduce bow-speed and pressure, then increase both speed and pressure *gradually* until you reach the end-note, in co-ordination with the sliding left-hand finger.

Indiscriminate use of the end-shift only cheapens it and robs it of its effectiveness. Whenever it is used, it should be remembered that it is not the shift itself which should be emphasized but the note to which it leads. It is that note whose expressive qualities should be enhanced and not the shift itself, which is merely the means toward that end.

Position Changes by Extension

The so-called 'positions', as they have been understood from the early eighteenth century, are convenient, but somewhat arbitrary and imaginary lines of demarcation on the fingerboard, similar to, but not as accurate as the line of the Equator on the Globe. In fact, a more logical division of the fingerboard, according to the definition of the location of the positions (the distance of the first finger from the nut) would be to say that there are as many positions on the fingerboard as there are half-steps: 24, instead of the customary seven positions. This would also fit in very well with the Tablature and System of Finger-patterns described earlier.

The left hand, depending on its size, can cover several 'positions' without moving: a tenth is really played in three positions at once:

(1st to 3rd)

and the famous 'Paganini chord' covers seven:

On the other hand, are these two differently notated notes:

really to be played in two different positions?

In any case, circumstances may make it preferable to reach a note outside the position by stretching, especially in technical passages:

Reaching a note by stretching can also render an expressive shift (which follows immediately from that note) more effective, especially if it goes in the opposite direction:

Concerto No. 2:
first movement   Vieuxtemps

Two consecutive expressive slides in opposite directions weaken and reduce their impact, and practically cancel each other out.

A GLOSSARY OF BOWING TERMS

The terminology of the various bowings is an area of some confusion and contradiction even among string players.

(1) Some general *musical* terms, when applied specifically to string playing, take on a different, specialized meaning. Terms such as 'staccato' and 'legato' denote not only the character of the sound, but also the means by which it is played on the instrument. Most composers used these terms in their musical meaning but, applied to string playing, they become *bowing* terms. (Conductors addressing the string section of an orchestra should be specific in the use of these terms: student conductors, please note!)

(2) In bowing terminology both Italian and French words are used and some of them—such as 'détaché'—are often incorrectly translated into English. Sometimes two different words—such as 'spiccato' and 'sautillé'—one Italian, one French, mean the same thing, but are translated as if they meant different bowings.

(3) Some terms—such as 'louré', 'portato' and 'collé'—indicate bowings which are only slight variations of one of the basic bowings, or on the borderline between two of them.

There are six fundamental bowings and they can be grouped into three pairs, each consisting of a single-note bowing (one note per bow) and a bowing of two or more notes per bow. In the following table, the first pair of bowings represent sustained notes, or notes of full sound duration ('tenuto', in its musical meaning); the second and third pairs include all the short notes, or notes of shortened sound duration (these are all staccato notes in the *musical* meaning of the term, but can be played on a string instrument by at least four different bowings, only one of which is called 'staccato' in bowing terminology, to mean a specific way to play short notes); the first and second pairs of bowings are on-string, the third pair off-string; the slight variants are given under the 'parent' basic bowing in the first five pairs, to unravel the confusion of (3) above.

The Basic Bowings and their Variants

(1) **Détaché (Fr.):**
(No It. used)

Single strokes, one note per bow, sustained and connected with no breaks or stops between notes. This is often translated incorrectly as 'detached', *ie* disconnected.

Variants:
Porté (Fr.) or **Portato (It.):**

Emphasis, or added inflection at the beginning of each détaché stroke.

Collé (Fr.)
(No It. used):

The long version of this bowing variant, basically an off-string détaché: the bow is slightly lifted between long notes; used in lower half.

(2) **Legato (It.):**
(No Fr. used)

Two or more notes on the same bow, tied or slurred uninterrupted. Often incorrectly translated to mean merely 'smooth'.

Variant:
Louré (Fr.):
(sometimes also Portato, It.)

A slightly articulated, pulsating legato.

(3) **Martelé (Fr.)**
Martellato (It.):

Short, single strokes, one note per bow, with stops between strokes. The bow usually moves rapidly and remains on string during the stops.

Variants:
Lancé (Fr.):
(No It. used)

Somewhat longer martelé (or somewhat shorter détaché), the bow faster at the beginning.

109

Collé (Fr.):
(No It. used)

Off-string martelé: short single notes pinched from the string, the bow off-string between notes.

Fouetté, or
Jeté (Fr.):

A short single note attacked from the air ('whipped', 'thrown' or 'slapped'), usually mixed with legato strokes, up-bow.

(4) Staccato (It.):
(No Fr. used)

A series of short notes, two or more per bow, separated by short stops, the bow remaining on string. (A series of martelé notes on the same bow.)

Variant:
Staccato Volante (It.) or
Staccato Volant (Fr.):

Similar to staccato, except bow is off-string between notes: 'flying staccato'.

(5) Spiccato (It.) or
Sautillé (Fr.):

Bouncing bow; short, single strokes, one note per bow, off-string between notes.

Variant:
'On-string' Spiccato (Eng.)
(No Fr. or It.):

High-speed spiccato with no time between the notes to bounce off-string. The hair remains mostly on-string, and the bow-stick oscillates slightly up and down.

(6) Saltato or Saltando (It.) or
Ricochet (Fr.):

Rebounding bow: two or more notes per bow, the bow rebounds between each note during the same bow as a result of the initial attack.

Since different bowings are often marked in the same way, the player must decide which specific ones to use on each occasion.